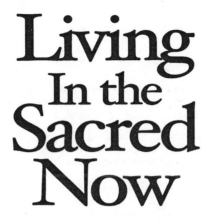

Living
In the
Sacred
Now

Kim Thomas

HARVEST HOUSE PUBLISHERS
Eugene, Oregon 97402

Cover photo by Philip Salaverry; Workbook Co/Op Stock

Cover by Left Coast Design, Portland, Oregon

LIVING IN THE SACRED NOW
Copyright © 2001 by Kim Thomas
Published by Harvest House Publishers
Eugene, Oregon 97402

Library of Congress Cataloging-in-Publication Data
Thomas, Kim, 1958-
   Living in the sacred now / Kim Thomas.
      p. cm.
   ISBN 0-7369-0529-4
   1. Meditations. 2. Christian life. I. Title.
   BV4832.3 .T48 2001
   242—dc21   2001016756

Printed in the United States of America.

01 02 03 04 05 06 07 08 09 10 / BC-BG / 10 9 8 7 6 5 4 3 2 1

To
Sid and Ann Wright

Train up a child in the way [she] should go,
and when [she] is old [she] will not depart from it.
Proverbs 22:6 NKJV

For this, and everything else, thank you.

Acknowledgments

Thank you, Terry Glaspey and Carolyn McCready, for believing in my work and nurturing it. For giving me a place to do what I love. The care that you and all the staff at Harvest House give extends my reach and fortifies me in the long hours.

Thank you, Sara Fortenberry, for finding me places.

Thank you to my family and friends who ask, "How's the book coming?" and really want to know.

Thank you, Dallas Willard, Cornelius Plantinga, Alister McGrath, Philip Yancey, Max Lucado, Anne Truitt (thanks, Hope), A. W. Tozer, Dan Allender, Tremper Longman, Kathleen Norris, Frederick Buechner, Annie Dillard, Francoise Fenelon, Ranier Maria Rilke, Anne Lamott, Evelyn Underhill, Thomas Merton, Henri Nouwen, The Desert Fathers, Robert Benson, G. Campbell Morgan, C. S. Lewis, Dorothy Sayers, and so many other authors for the words between the covers.

Thank you to my husband, Jim, for walking a few steps ahead of me, for pursuing Christ with hunger, for editing and encouraging, for gathering me up when I crumble, for studying me and then loving me with an intentional heart.

Contents

"'If any man open the door, I will come in to him';
share his ordinary meal, and irradiate his ordinary life. The
demand for temperance of soul, for acknowledgment of the
sacred character of the normal, is based on that fact—the
central Christian fact—of the humble entrance of
God into our common human life."

Evelyn Underhill
House of the Soul and Concerning the Inner Life

The In-Between

Sometimes I think about running away to the circus. It's not too late. I keep a bag in the basement in case I need to pack quickly. Sometimes the seriousness of life makes me hungry for the complete fantasy of the circus. I can't resist the feats of strength and daring to which the performers give themselves so relentlessly.

What woos me most is the flying trapeze act. It is so all or nothing. There is no room for halfway commitment or apathetic involvement. Spandex-and-sequin costumed bodies are suspended from delicate bars at the top of the tent. They have rehearsed their act, so with grace and timing, toes pointed, they leap fearlessly from one bar to the next. But the time between the bars is not dead time. It is the peak of the performance. They throw themselves across the upper regions of the Big Top with triple somersaults and half twists, unfolding just in time to catch the next bar. Flying. That's what those trapeze people do between the bars. I want to fly too.

I can see the next trapeze bar I am to jump toward in my life, but timing is everything. If I let go and reach for the next one too soon, I will fall. If I wait too long, my chance is passed. But in the time between this trapeze bar and the next, there is a leap of faith that will set me flying.

My problem is that I keep thinking the only safe places are the two swinging bars. The time between them is unknown and risky. Perhaps the secret would be to swing long and hard enough on one bar until one could hold both this bar and the next one. But then there would be no flying. And flying is where life is fully lived, where progress is made, and where the view is the best.

Life is a series of in-betweens. Between here and there, between being born and dying. Between doubt and faith, between night and day, between coming and going. Life gives us so many opportunities for feeling in-between. For people of faith, life is ultimately a collection of in-betweens that symbolize our passage from justification through sanctification and on to glorification. From redemption to completion. That's what makes the flight so compelling. The opportunity to find wonder in the midst of our everyday lives transforms the agony of the struggle into the adventure of becoming.

We are between one thing and another on a daily basis. If we train ourselves to become aware, to pay close attention, we'll find messages in every moment. Messages of guidance, comfort, peace, growth, promise, wisdom, perspective, rest. They are best found by occupying the moment. One does well to dwell. Perseverance through the in-between times may cause us to go a little slower, breathe a little deeper, see a bit more, and notice the "not by chance" moments. At times our progress may seem slow, but it is in this collection of in-betweens, one slightly perceptible step after another, that we become. Doubt becomes faith, night becomes morning, caterpillars get wings.

Overly concerned with what has been, stressed and consumed by what is yet to be, we tend to forget that life is happening in the immediacy of this instant. The invitation of this book is to the "now." In surrender to the Spirit, now can become more than a holding pattern, a painful pause, or a frightening flight. It can become important. Significant. Fulfilling. Extraordinary.

Sacred.

1

Between Water and Wine

~

*W*hen the first dry leaves begin to be dragged into my house by the two miniature schnauzer princesses who own the place, I know cold weather is planning her next visit. Before I start to get cranky, anticipating miserable cold and cursed wind, I try to coerce myself into a good attitude. I make the first pot of fall tea.

Typically I like it to be a cup of the black currant herbal tea Jim and I discovered on a trip to London. The smell seems to take me to a place of contentment. It is a positive reminder that in the death that comes with fall, there is some good to be found. Well, tea at least. I like all the seasons, it's just that winter is my least favorite and fall means winter is next. I suppose I blame fall by its close proximity, at least for the first couple of weeks. So I have had to devise some rituals of redemption for my yearly anticipation of what lies ahead.

The process of making a pot of tea helps to ease me into the pace of fall. Like a hibernating bear, my breathing and heart slow down so as to conserve energy for the next season. I clean out the tea cupboard and dispose of old tea, making room for new flavors I plan on discovering. And each fall, I buy myself a new teacup, designated as this year's favorite. Sometimes it is an old antique cup with a delicate matching plate that I indulge in, and sometimes it is a mug that looks as though it came from a donut shop, pragmatic and sturdy. It just depends on my mood. And what I find.

To steep tea is to immerse the leaves and imbue their flavor to the water. Sometimes I make a pot with a couple of bags tethered to the handle, and sometimes I like to suspend the leaves in a press pot. But either way, the essence of the leaf is not fully passed into the water unless the steep is at least three minutes. And it can take up to five or seven minutes for some teas. If my pulse is 80 beats a minute, then for a small leaf tea my heart will beat 240 times while it steeps. My lungs will fill with air and then relinquish that air 36 times, unless I begin to get overly anxious, which I usually do. Then I end up drinking a pale version of tea that my most devoted tea friends scoff at. So I try to wait. Between water and tea.

When my husband Jim and I were in France for our twentieth wedding anniversary, we discovered that wine was cheaper than Coca-Cola. And for the good reason of being frugal, we developed a liking for various French table wines. One local wine stormed our taste buds so dramatically that we decided we wanted to visit the vineyard where the grapes were grown and the fermentation took place. Kindly, the wine steward at Le Chevre D'Or peeled the label off the bottle and glued it to a card from the restaurant so that we could remember Chateau Minuty. "A modest white wine."

We ventured the French highways west from where we were staying on the southern coast and eventually wandered down four different incorrect dirt roads until we found the Chateau Minuty vineyards. The two and a half hours of driving netted an anti-climactic view of a small and humble vineyard. But we were allowed to wander unaccompanied on the grounds, so we squeezed as much adventure out of it as we could. We surveyed the ordered rows of vines sporting green leaves and no fruit at this time. The stalks themselves were appropriately knotty and crooked, like in movies. We stooped to touch the dirt, wondering what nutrients were required for such special grapes, and then found our way back to the main barn where the vats were located.

A simple one-page handout described the process of fermentation that was taking place in the tanks and barrels. Water turning to wine takes much longer than water turning to tea. Before the fruit ever reaches the vats, water that falls from the sky makes a genial collaboration with the soil, sun, and vines during the growing season and eventually becomes juice within the ripe fruit. There are many varieties of grapes, but it is only the charmingly named "noble grapes" that will make the best wine.

When noble grapes are ripe, as determined by the experienced grower, they are harvested for juicing. Then grape juice is turned into alcohol by the process of fermentation. Waiting. Between water and wine is fermentation. Waiting. I want to taste the liquid that is mid-ferment to see how well it weathers the in-between. Does it taste more like juice or wine? When does it make the change that matures it into value? Do I recognize that moment in my own maturing, my own fermenting?

With much time, water will become wine. But my heart would beat and my lungs would fill too many times to count and my impatience with steeping tea would be outdone by my impatience with the fermentation of grapes.

There once was a wine that did not need time to ferment.

This is the life I would like to select for myself please, one where change and fermenting is instantaneous and effortless. At a wedding in Cana sat six large stone water pots. They each held between 20 and 30 gallons of water for the required ceremonial cleansings at this Jewish wedding ceremony. The water was kept nearby, fortunately convenient for Jesus to use as an unexpected provision.

Mary, the mother of Jesus, was evidently much involved in the goings on of this wedding. Jesus and a few of His disciples were also in attendance. But whether the guests were drinking more than expected, or whether more guests than expected had arrived, the wine began to run out. Before the guests could find out about the embarrassing wine emergency, Mary appealed to her Son to do something. Some have said this was the presumptuous request of a mere woman to her miracle-working Son from heaven, but I see instead a busy mother delegating to a capable son. It was as absurd for her to direct the Heir of heaven as it is for us to dictate to Him how and when He is to work in our lives. She simply made Him aware, responded to the servants saying, "do whatever He asks," and didn't give it another thought. She doesn't direct Jesus to make wine or make the guests go home; she confidently leaves the task to His judgment.

I don't often confidently leave my requests in the throne room with that kind of complete trust. I would like to direct and suggest how to choreograph the sudden crisis in my life, with a tight fist clenched around "my way." But Christ is the Christ, God very God, and He is competent to the job.

Expediently and confidently, Jesus performs the first miracle as a sign. It was not for the crowds to see and be awed, but for those behind the scenes to believe. He instructed the servants to fill the water pots and then serve some to the head steward. Jesus did not wave over the water pots or even command the water to be wine. He did not wait for it to steep three minutes. He did not wait for the rain to fall and the vines to ripen and the juice to ferment. In an unceremonious moment, this One who was there when the Father created cosmos out of nothing, decided that something could be so, and it was so. Should we be surprised?

Water became wine.

The steward was impressed with the flavor of the wine, but even more with the bridegroom for bringing out the best at the last. Most people served the best wine first, so that after their guests' tastes were not quite as discriminating, they wouldn't notice the decline in the quality of the wine. But here we have the unexpected, brought about by the Son of God. When God transforms, He makes the best. He doesn't just provide what is adequate for the moment, but the taste of heaven intended for our best.

It is not the design of Christ to take away our humanity, but to sanctify it. When water would have quenched, He gave wine. One of the first miracles that Moses performed to urge Pharaoh to free his people was to turn water into blood. In contrast, the Savior's first miracle was to turn water into wine, symbolizing the new covenant He came to establish. No longer would blood quench the thirst for sanctification. The grace of new wine would.

Sometimes water becomes tea in three minutes. Sometimes water becomes wine in a few years. And once and maybe sometimes, in a Jesus-directed moment, water becomes wine instantly. Augustine has said that just as Christ made wine in those six water pots on that day, He does the same every year with the vines. What the clouds spill is changed into wine by that same direction of heaven. Sometimes change is instant at the Master's touch, other times change takes a very long time. Miracles convey the power of God, but time conveys the grace.

Notice that what the servants put into the water pots was changed in its very essence by the doings of the Lord. What do I put in my water pots to be transformed, fermented?

Are the tea leaves in my life something worth imbuing into my soul?

May I fill my pots to overflowing. May I pour into them my efforts, longings, strivings, hopes, and my will. I can bring my humble, everyday water for purification and wait for it to become the wine of celebration. And may I have grace to endure the steeping, the fermenting, for however long He chooses.

I keep my teacups next to my wine glasses in my cupboard. This wasn't intentional, but I'm glad I do. I line them all up in corresponding shapes and sizes, leaving them at the ready for when I need to pour water that transforms. It reminds me that transformations and in-betweens last for varying times, but that the resulting savor will have the distinct taste of heaven.

2

Between
Young and Old

~

Midlife is the place where our former sense of our own immortality collides with the realization that we will one day be a statistic on the obituary page. The panic we feel over this is what we call the "midlife crisis." And the probability of everyone experiencing some version of this crisis is more than high.

The inevitability of life, age, change, wounds, and death seems to speak louder than the possibility of dreams, expectations, and unknown adventures. Our failing and sagging bodies cause us to avoid mirrors. The mountains we've climbed have brought us to a view revealing only higher mountains. Relationships begin to seem homogenous and unsatisfying. The burden of depression weighs us down and we wonder if we have spent ourselves in a valuable enough way to give our life meaning. Something whispers in our ear: What does it matter anyway?

My skin just doesn't fit as well as it used to. And my confidence slips more than it doesn't. Sometimes it feels as though I'm in a deep sleep and someone is calling out to me. I'm trying to surface but can't get my mind to tell my body to wake up. It's as though I am behind a glass wall seeing my life, but I'm not in it. Nothing turned out the way I thought it would. Somewhere along the way, I lost myself.

Midlife introduces us to someone we haven't met before—the older version of ourselves.

This older version of ourselves needs new purpose because by this time in life, we tend to have run out of vision. Without vision, the people perish. Sometimes we feel as though we are perishing. The vision of the past years doesn't fit the newer and older us. We have to be in search of new visions, but the only way to discover a new vision is to get to know who we are now, where we want to go, and what we want to be.

People used to ask us what we wanted to be when we grew up. The problem is that we are grown up now, and the dreams and goals of childhood don't feel roomy enough anymore. But no one seems to ask us what we want to be when we are *more* grown up. It's as if we had one chance, and now it's over. So what are we supposed to do with all the other years ahead of us? A change of perspective sees them as full of possibility, and perhaps second chances. A chance for more dreaming and becoming.

We have to learn to see the future as simply the next phase instead of just what's left. When I spend a dollar bill and get back 30 cents change, I don't just consider the dollar spent. I know that I can buy something else with the 30 cents I have left. The narrow vision of our youth needs some adjusting and tailoring to whom we have become, so that we realize there is plenty of us left to spend.

This midlife time is a chance for us to catch our breath, plan, meditate, intensify. Plato said, "The spiritual eyesight improves as the physical eyesight declines." This is not the beginning of the end, or the end of the beginning. This is a season for seeing in a new way.

Our culture would have us seeing through eyes that tell us we are spent and past our prime. That's why we so desperately try to tuck in the flesh hanging over the edges of all our garments and stand in front of the mirror pulling and pushing our face, simulating the possible benefits of surgery. That we would even consider allowing someone to slice open the face we have known for over 40 years is evidence of the strong intoxicant of youth. We need to see this midlife with new spiritual eyes.

"People judge by the outer appearance, but God looks at the heart."

This paraphrase of 1 Samuel 16:7 is not meant to patronize our insecurities or place a Band-Aid on our hemorrhaging heart. It is the foundation of the new improved spiritual eyesight that is offered us.

"The godly shall flourish...even in old age they will still produce fruit and be vital..." (Psalm 92:12-14 TLB).

This psalm is the promise of vision. To no longer be vital is the most eminent fear of the midlifer. Does anyone need or want me now, or am I just the husk, what's left when the good stuff is taken? George Eliot said "It is never too late to be what you might have been." The words from the psalmist and Ms. Eliot are the balm that soothes the ache of unmet expectations, giving us courage to see a future.

Recovering and restarting the soul takes time. So start with a really good sigh. Breathe in the sacred now, and breathe deeply. Exhale the disappointments and the worn-out soul you've been trying to live in. Let your shoulders rise and fall with the Gloria Patri, the Introit to a new season. "As it was in the beginning, is now and ever shall be, world without end…"

So what resonates with you? What do you want to plant in your soul today? Enjoy a moment of quiet to listen. Stop being busy. A great pianist said that it isn't just the notes played that make music, it is also the pauses between the notes. Enjoy the pause of midlife.

And when the pause has given you the strength to dream and plan again, do.

In her late 70s, Anna Mary Robertson Moses took up painting because her hands were too arthritic to continue embroidering. Three years later, Grandma Moses, the self-taught primitive painter of rural life, enjoyed her first solo show at the Gallerie Saint Etienne in New York City.

Margaret Fogarty Rudkin began baking bread for her son because of his allergies to commercially processed bread. In her 40s, suddenly the redheaded, middle-aged mother had a valuable business. In 1960, she sold Pepperidge Farm to Campbell Soup for millions.

Sarah was almost 100 years old when she and Abraham gave birth to Isaac, the father of the nation of Israel.

Moses was in his 80s when he switched career directions from shepherd to nation-leader, when he helped emancipate the Israelites and lead them to freedom.

The *puya raimondii* is the slowest blooming plant in the world. This bromeliad is 150 years old before flowers appear.

"Is not wisdom found among the aged? Does not long life bring understanding?" (Job 12:12).

Midlife is the opportunity to meet a second self, a fuller version of *you*. Robert Browning wrote, "The best is yet to be, the last of life, for which the first was made." Now is the time to invest in the things that you will not regret. And whether your contribution is legendary in history or simply a faithful life well lived, it is a time of opportunity. Opportunity to see things in a new way. To observe and pay attention.

To bloom.

3

Between Egypt and the Promised Land

~

My throat is dry. My soul is thirsty. The dust collects heavy in my eyelashes and burns my eyes.

This is wilderness. But though I am in exile, I am not abandoned. If I will place myself on the path of obedience, there will be manifestations of the Divine Presence to guide me. Sometimes, if I squint, I can barely make out a cloud that urges me forward.

What is a wilderness experience? Fundamentally, it is a rescue from slavery with the promise of a future. It is a time of preparation. A time of molding and testing. A time of God's provision and protection. A time of learning and establishing a life of faith built on obedience and trust, all in anticipation of entering His presence.

23

It can also be a time of drought. Drudging routine. Confusion. Desert walking. And walking. And more walking.

Our time of wilderness is the most defining in-between time we will experience. It is in general a time of trial that is distinguished by the feeling that we are adrift from the familiar safety zones of our life. It may also be a time of geographical abandonment or emotional abandonment, when friends or loved ones are no longer available to us. Many times, the familiar things that bring us comfort—actual material things or places or routines—are no longer available or accessible.

We can see this time as stimulating and new and embrace the drought, finding sacred spaces and moments in new places. Or, even though we know this is a time of rescue and renewal, we can look over our shoulder and long for the onions and fleshpots of Egypt. We can find ourselves unsatisfied and whining, which are eminent signs of rebellion.

Moses led the Israelites through the most well-known wilderness experience in all of history. A rescue from slavery to Pharaoh and the Egyptians with a destination of the Promised Land, which should have been a very short trip, became a lifetime journey that few of the participants completed.

There were so many temper tantrums and riotous whinings over circumstances and leadership that God chose to keep them circling in the wilderness, in a time-out if you will, until they learned a faithful dependence on the God of deliverance. They were given distinct forms of guidance in the pillar of cloud by day and the pillar of fire by night, and distinct provision in daily manna. They were delivered from slavery and battle. God's faithfulness in the face of their faithlessness showed the ultimate failure of their hearts and the relentless mercy of the One who led them.

They were continually unsatisfied with the provision of food, so God finally consented to give them quails to eat. After insistent grumbling about water, instead of lecturing them about His previous deliverance and constant care for them, He brought water out of a rock for them.

Psalm 106 says "He gave them their request, but sent leanness into their souls." Sometimes in our wilderness, when we are given what we ask for, the foolishness of our hearts is revealed to us.

In their disobedience, the people created for themselves a golden calf to worship. A symbol of their ultimate willfulness, this was conceived while Moses was up on the mountain receiving the word of the Lord, a covenant that would make them conscious of their need for the holiness of God.

There was collateral to be paid. And people died. And in that moment, it would seem that the patience of God was tried and His heart was broken.

He remained faithful to care for and lead His people, but they never again adorned themselves with ornaments of joy in the wilderness. Disobedience thwarts joy.

Disobedience and unbelief are revealed in the wilderness. Dissatisfaction can keep us wandering longer than we were intended to. Even when the people were in sight of the Promised Land, they refused to believe God would deliver it to them because of their fears of the unknown. Fear of the unknown can keep us from moving forward.

If we cling to the present or past and refuse to trust Him for the future, if we are blind to the sacred now, we'll be denied entrance to the presence of God. Canaan. The Promised Land. The ultimate communion.

This is the point where the wilderness showdown occurs. Do we trust God to give us the future, or do we rely on our own fallible reasoning? It is so hard to believe and trust that God will deliver us when all of our senses say otherwise. Proverbs 14 can bring us a pause for wisdom, for "there is a way that seems right to [us,] but in the end it leads to death." Our senses are unreliable. We must trust God for our deliverance.

How long do we really want to be between Egypt and the Promised Land?

God's original design was for a shorter trip through the wilderness. The manna He fed the people with was enough to sustain but not satisfy them. They were only a short journey away from the lush and abundant food of promise. But disobedience meant 40 years of dining on manna.

I am a short journey away from more than satisfaction. In my wilderness I can trust God to be faithful and dig down deep for water, or I can surrender to my instinct to whine and rebel. But it will cost. God will allow me to rebel and wrestle for control until I come to the end of my own self. And then, when I have surrendered to obedience, sometimes after 40 years, He will carry me into the land of promise.

Plants can survive desert life by preserving water or by developing extensive root systems. One plant that has developed both survival techniques is the creosote bush. It drops or folds its leaves to preserve water and sends out root systems able to go deep into the water table. It propagates itself by sending shoots out which develop their own roots and branches which are genetically identical to the original bush. A grouping like this was found in the Mojave Desert and is dated at approximately 11,700 years old. It is the oldest plant life yet known. A wilderness survivor.

We would do well to shed unnecessary things and develop deep spiritual roots if we are to survive our own wilderness experiences.

The name of the bush is inspired by the odor it puts out, an odor similar to creosote. Creosote is a liquid that is created from wood tar, the carbonization, or burning, of wood. It is used extensively for pharmaceutical healing purposes.

It is interesting that Moses' initial invitation to the wilderness journey was delivered by a bush, a burning bush whose name was "I Am That I Am."

4

Between
Doubt and Faith

~

Seasons of doubt feel dark and foreboding. It's as if clouds and darkness have replaced the sureness of daylight. In that claustrophobic cloud of unknowing, I am suffering what many fathers and mothers of the faith have called the dark night of the soul. It is the place between the known and the unknown, the place where my confidence in the things I knew to be true melts like a whisper, where the candlelight of truth seems snuffed out. I am afflicted by the shadow of doubt.

Did I get here by binding up my doubts with invisible threads that break at the first tug? Or by eating yesterday's rations of truth instead of disciplining myself for daily manna? I am often guilty of laziness and under-believing, but does that have to leave me marooned in the dark?

In our lives there are things that are expressible and there are things that are unspeakable. The unspeakables often become speakable only after a long gestation in the dark.

It's amazing how you can have everything buzzing along, and then one day wake up to discover, like St. John of the Cross, your "house being now all stilled." It's not that you have let loose of the truth that tethers your soul to Christ, it's just that everything has gone quiet. And dark.

Someone has suggested that doubt is faith's shadow. It is the darkness on the other side of light. Which is also to say that you can't doubt if you haven't got faith. That is reassuring. But in the hush that dampens my spirit, I long for more than that. I want to see once again the things I once saw so clearly. St. John of the Cross says that the dark night of the soul is a "dense and burdensome cloud which afflicts the soul and keeps it withdrawn from God." But in the midst of that darkness, interior transformation can begin.

From where I sit, the clouds are rolling in.

Madeleine L'Engle has written that faith isn't a magic charm we can wave at our problems or doubts to chase them away. Instead it is what will sustain us through those times. Faith will be the night light that gets me through the night terrors.

I do know that the dark nights eventually yield growth. As I've grown older, I've grown a little more patient for the ripening of my faith. Solitude is no longer a threat of loneliness, but a gift of contemplation. I find that embracing the dark times is the best way to grow. John Powell has said "one thing is certain, that passage through the darkness of doubts and crises, however painful it may be, is essential to growth in the process of faith."

What is it about the dark that yields growth?

Seeds lie dormant until they are in the right condition for germination. From the outside they show no signs of life. But put them under the dark cover of soil in close proximity to water, oxygen, and proper temperature—things begin to change. Germination is the commencement of growth. The embryo's cell enlarges and splits open the hardened seed coat, allowing a root and a shoot to emerge. From this point on, the roots will grow and develop in the darkness while the shoot containing the leaves and stem will flourish above ground in the light. But even if the stem is bruised, or the plant withers, strong roots below will cause it to sprout new growth, again.

In the dark night of my soul, I am a candidate for the commencement of growth. If, as I wait in the dark, in the quiet uncertainty, I will feed myself the proper soul nourishment, the hard shell of my heart will be broken and exposed. It is only then that I can begin to grow new roots that will sustain me despite the bruising and withering I will endure.

In the book, *The Cloud of Unknowing,* the unknown author offers the hope that it will be in the Father's will to send out a ray of spiritual light to melt the cloud of unknowing between us and Him, and that He will share with us some of the unspeakables. And then, "you shall feel your affection all aflame with the fire of His love."

That would warm the chill left from the darkness.

When, as Eugene Peterson says, "doubt forces faith to bedrock," I have a choice to make. I can fold my hands and crumble, deciding this is all too hard for me. Or I can burrow deeper, growing roots and reaching my hands up to the light. If I choose the latter, I will discover the grasp of the Faithful Savior reaching out for me. And I will be wrapped up and enfolded in His love, gathered again and again.

This decision can't be trusted to just my feelings, because I will often feel like crumbling instead of pressing in. It takes discipline to walk through the dark night of the soul. And there will be more than one. I want to race to the end of the darkness and find the security of His light as soon as humanly possible. But I won't find the way through by trusting in human possibilities or running fast. Rainer Maria Rilke encourages us to be patient and learn to live the questions. Then perhaps gradually, without being aware of it, we will live along into the answers.

In the words of Isaiah 50:10, "Let him who walks in the dark, who has no light, trust in the name of the LORD."

5

Between Mentors

~

*J*n pursuit of an art degree, I sharpened each eraser-less pencil with a hand sharpener and then used a sandpaper paddle to keep them sharp. I had a properly kneaded eraser, pliable and ready to serve. The tools for drawing, including an 18 x 24 newsprint pad, were tucked under my arm as I made my way across campus to the second semester of drawing class. Still early in my core curriculum classes, I felt more myself than I had in a long time.

A math major until my junior year of college, I finally experienced a moment of coming to my senses. What had I been thinking? I was young; there was still plenty of time. After a trip to the registrar's office, I was set, no longer lost in a pursuit that didn't fit me. I was now an art major, and I loved the tools of my new craft, the smudges of graphite on my fingers, the surface of a fine rag paper.

For one of the assignments in Drawing II, we were told to find a drawing by one of the great masters and copy it line for line. I tracked down a copy of a self-portrait of Rembrandt. HB pencil in hand, I began to lose myself in the maze of short, long, curved, and straight lines that led me around his face. At first I saw just lines. But then the lines began to work together, and I saw the bottom and one side of a triangle joined by a half circle which became the side view of an eye. A gently arcing line indicated the bridge of a nose, and a sort of lazy, stretched-out "M" became the top lips of a mouth.

By studying Rembrandt and other masters, I learned how they solved drawing challenges and added to my own visual vocabulary.

I would like to have that same sort of reference for my life as a woman of faith. The journey of faith is not always a clearly mapped trip, but there are ways we can see more clearly by following in the footsteps of someone who is further down the road. At first they are just footprints, but then they begin to join together to form a path. And so we add to our own spiritual vocabulary.

I've had a lot of mentors. Some were professional, inspiring me to do good work. Others were relational, modeling marriage and friendship. My mom is one of them; certainly she's number one on my speed dial. She walks me through many of my struggles. But sometimes moms are too close to help you see objectively.

Right now, I am between mentors. I long for someone here in my own town, a woman older than me who can model spiritual faithfulness as well as the realities of falling down and getting back up. Someone who will feel the freedom to be corrective and challenging with me.

I've considered advertising.

I need someone to help me figure things out. How do you handle the days of contentment that suddenly, with no transitional grace, become days of unspeakable sadness? And what about the days when your self-esteem is so low that you walk through the mall screaming "see me" in your heart to the strangers that walk by? And how do you balance having and wanting lovely things with the guilt of seeing a homeless man sleeping slumped against the side of the bus station?

What about marriage and family issues? The things you can only know after being married for 20 years or more. How do you navigate midlife with your partner? How do you plan for and anticipate your parents' elder years?

Where is the woman who can help me walk through these seasons? Who can help bridge my youth and my womanhood?

Community is an essential in the life of faith. Dr. Paul Brand says that all cells in our body function in an interdependent way. The only cells that act independently are cancer cells.

No wonder Christ compared the church to a body.

If the church is to function like a healthy body, we must live interdependently. But this will involve a certain amount of vulnerability and honesty. And a recognition that we need some help from each other. It's easier to avoid the exposure involved in such contact, but then we miss the intimate experience of community found in mentoring relationships.

I don't think I would ever have thought of copying the masters as a way to learn to draw. I probably would have been afraid it would be seen as a cheater's way to shortcut the system. It's easy to carry that kind of thinking over into living out our lives. We fear that if we don't find our way on our own, we will be seen as weak, as looking for the easy way out.

But that kind of attitude negates the wisdom of experience we can glean from another's well-lived life. Learning from their mistakes and successes can have an exponential effect. We observe, apply, and live, and then others observe us, apply, and live, and so on.

So I'm looking. I'm looking for gray hair, or discreetly colored gray hair. I'm looking for smile wrinkles, hands that are comfortable in dirt or pearls, an easy laugh, knees worn from time spent on them, a well-used Bible, and a wing looking for someone to take under it.

I'm looking for a great master of faith whose lines I can copy.

6

Between
Naked and Clothed

~

What does it mean when you have a recurring dream that you have gone someplace and suddenly discover that you are naked?

I've had this dream three times in the last month. Each time I am out somewhere and everything is going along fine. Then, all of a sudden, I realize that I am ensemble-less and scramble to find a shred of cloth or a napkin to discreetly disguise my vulnerability as I sneak out the back door or crawl under a table.

I remember a time when I was six and my father was giving me my nightly bath. After I had baptized all of my dolls, Dad soaped up the washcloth to help remove the day's grime from my skin, then pulled the plug and grabbed a towel for me. It was at this point that I said, "Dad, you have to go now because you can't see me naked."

What causes us to realize our nakedness? When does it go from ok to not ok?

The day in the Garden when Eve and Adam chose to eat of the fruit of the forbidden tree, they discovered their nakedness. For a long eternal moment they had enjoyed the Garden in their unadorned bare-ness. It was beautiful, and they were unaware of their exposure. But awareness and conscience were born when the fruit was eaten. Disobedience brought forth shame. In shame and regret they hid themselves from God, their Father and Friend, because of their new, sudden knowledge.

Since that defining moment, we've been trying to clothe ourselves. To cover the shame.

Easter was always a fashion fling at our house. My mom and sister and I would enjoy the annual spring rite of shopping for Easter Sunday outfits. One year the money was not there for our usual shopping trip. Mom and my sister could make do with what they had, but I'd grown beyond the hem of most of my clothes. Well, I can count on one hand the number of things my mother has sewn over the years. Only if she was absolutely unable to staple, glue, or pin, would she face the monster and break out the Singer. But that spring called for just such desperate measures.

There was not even money for fabric. Mom's ingenuity and eye for transformation led her to pull down the antique midnight blue satin curtains from her bedroom windows. A near nervous breakdown later, the fabric that had gone in one end of the sewing machine as curtains, came out the other end a smart-looking-dress-and-jacket combo. Easter morning I stood a proud 39" tall in my new outfit for family pictures.

Remember, it was also spring when the Savior fashioned our clothes for us. On Friday before the first Easter, in the moment Christ was providing the righteousness for us to be clothed in, He hung naked and alone before a dark world.

Vulnerable and exposed. Dressed only in the shame and regret of humanity.

In the moment that it was finished, the Father ripped down His own curtain that we might have access to Him because of Jesus, our covering garment.

Jesus' death and resurrection changed the destiny of the naked human heart. A people separated from God, uncovered and shamed by their faithless acts, in need of a way to approach Him again, were clothed in the righteousness of Christ.

Today I sat on my porch fully clothed. As I felt the heat of the day fade to dusk, there was a chill that I could not shake. A cup of tea and my old-man cardigan sweater with its two moth holes didn't warm me up. The chill was deeper than that. I was sensing again the condition of my heart, bare and peeled back and raw to the expensive emotions that come with the package of who I am. The weakness of my resolve always surprises me. I try to clothe my heart in good work, to be creative and deliberate. The pages of my life speak like the rings of growth in an exposed tree, chronicling the days of faithfulness and faithlessness, the days of effort at self-massage. "You are good because you do good work," I tell myself. Exposed by my desire to eat from the forbidden tree, I long to be self-sufficient in my daily survival and in the covering of my nakedness.

But my old-man cardigan sweater will never cover my need. Neither will anything else in my self-sustaining wardrobe.

As evening is swallowing what is left of the day, I go inside and walk from room to room, closing the curtains. They will stay closed another night, sheltering me from the darkness on the other side.

7

Between Burning Bushes

~

I'm a pretty decisive person. I have opinions on just about everything. They aren't all informed or spoken with erudition, but I'll venture to offer my thoughts if asked.

Decisions are actually a fairly even risk. It's "a" or "b," 50=50, win or lose. When you boil it down to a worst-case scenario, things begin to simplify. Trauma at the mall: black open-toed sandals or red suede driving moccasins? Prices are within quarters, both are comfortable. Should I be practical and get the sandals that go with everything, or spend a wild card and get happy shoes? What's the worst thing that can happen? I'll have the wrong shoes to wear with my whatever. Decision made; it's the moccasins.

That was easy. Most of my decisions carry nonthreatening collateral when it comes right down to it. But on occasion, I long for a burning bush calling or two. I know what they look like. I've warmed my hands at one and been singed by a couple over the years. I've only seen their distinct glow a handful of times, but after the first one, you begin to get better at seeing them.

Ok, sometimes it isn't burning bushes, but maybe smoking leaves, or glowing embers, or a small clump of self-combusting weeds. But the guidance is still there to be found. I prefer the fully flaming bush of fire, but God sends those sparingly. He equipped us with firing neurons in a complex brain enhanced with five senses—six if you're a woman—to inform our thinking. The sparks from these are strong indicators for our decision-making process.

I also find that the glow generated on the faces of people who know and love me can be a light for my life. When I'm not certain about a direction, I'll run it past a few key counselors and see what lights up. Usually there is a consensus that I can store in my mental file.

For people of faith, Scripture and prayer are key sources for discerning direction. At this point, I'm not talking about buying shoes or choosing hair color. It's not that God doesn't care (I mean, I'm sure He'd have an opinion), but probably He doesn't *really* care in the omnipotent, omniscient, Godhead sort of way. My understanding is that He knows and cares about how many hairs are on my head and that, yes He clothes the lily, so how much more will He clothe me. But what He really desires for me in all decisions is that they, in some way, help me to better love the Lord my God with all my heart, soul, strength, and mind, and love my neighbor as myself.

With that as a paradigm, the demand for burning bushes should be reduced significantly.

But there are still times when, in spite of all the equipping He has done, I need a bit of divine guidance to confirm my more significant decisions. I long for the face-to-face, face-to-burning-bush, face-to-"pillar of cloud by day and pillar of fire by night" kind of guidance.

As in when I think of career transitions, for example. I mean, that's when Moses got a burning bush. He was a shepherd and was being promoted to Acting Director of God's People to and Through the Wilderness. He was given bushes, clouds, manna, and rocks that spit water, not to mention the Ten Commandments. All I'm asking for is just a little sparkler-like ragweed.

How does one make a life change as big as this without looking for a distinct sign from heaven? When you've invested your life and self in something, and then begin to feel the joy and satisfaction wane, change is near. The fulfillment that used to send you blissfully off to live for Him has changed into obligation and a list of "shoulds" and "have tos." Bliss becomes a distant memory and you feel the opposite of what Dorothy Sayers felt when she said "true love knows no suffering." What I have done for so many years often no longer feels like true love. And vocations can change. I find myself imagining other scenarios where I would feel more efficiently applied. And all of the symptoms are present for change.

So I bury myself in prayer and Scripture meditation. I consult my wisest, most insightful counselors. I tune into circumstances. I weigh pros and cons and project worst-case scenarios. And while I'm looking for fire, in a subtle and noncombustible way my spirit finds peace that passes understanding.

There isn't always an audible voice or a skywritten message, but every moment I spend in the presence of God I am standing on holy ground, and it leaves the sweet smell of God-fire on me. And an impression of direction begins to come into focus.

I think the thing about burning bushes is that maybe they don't show up the way they used to. We are thinking too literally, too much like Charlton Heston in the *Ten Commandments*. Elizabeth Barrett Browning said "Earth's crammed with heaven, and every common bush afire with God; but only he who sees takes off his shoes, the rest sit round and pluck blackberries." We look at burning bushes all the time, but we don't see them. I'm looking for the ones that have been trimmed and cut in the shape of words with little flames on the tops of them. But His signature is on every bush and tree, His guidance is available, and I should take off my shoes.

So I remove the asbestos suit and goggles, and sit in the eternal now, attuned to every common bush. And if He chooses, I am prepared for the extraordinary bush. While I wait I try to attune my heart and eyes to pay attention to more subtle guidance. Patience in the Presence will bring—if not flaming bushes—at least glowing hearts.

8

Between
"This Little Light" and
"I'm Gonna Let It Shine"

~

First of all, I don't feel shine-ish. And secondly, if God gave me said light, it isn't going to be little.

It's going to be a big searchlight blasting a luminescence that consumes every dark corner. Right now, however, I have the dimmer switch on. I'm waiting for a good dark moment to blast the light into.

Anyone searching nearby will just have to stumble their way around until I feel shine-ish again. And besides, I'm not the only searchlight out there. I shouldn't be expected to be on duty nonstop, should I?

Jim and I were driving home from dinner the other night, and as we pulled into our driveway I saw the lights of summer come on. Marauding through the air of my front yard at two minutes past dusk were the floating and well-choreographed moves of the *pyropyga*, literally translated, "fire rump."

Their ballet was delicate and constant, no one firefly demanding more attention than another. Just when you would locate one of them, their light would dim and they would blend into the sky and pass the torch to the next flyer.

When I was of firefly-catching age, I would capture them gently, sometimes getting "light" on my fingers. Historically, they are willing hostages, living out many days in empty mayonnaise jars with holes punched in the lids. I tried to feed them red Kool-Aid once, to try and make their lights red. Evidently they don't care for Kool-Aid.

I sort of wish, for their sake, that they were "fire heads" instead of "fire rumps." They could see where they were going then, instead of where they had been. But you deal with what you've got.

These little night-lights have light-producing organs containing a chemical called "luciferin." (No association to what you might be thinking.) When luciferin combines with air, the abdomen glows and we see light. Most of them use this light to attract potential mates to themselves or to warn predators of their bitter taste. Fireflies have species-specific light patterns that identify them, and they can take the form of anything from a constant glow to discrete blinking to multipulsed flashes. Ballet, ballroom, and disco.

The once and for all purpose of their lights has been debated. But I can't help but think what the purpose of a light is, except to show the way. In this case, to show the way to the light performance of the firefly.

I find them enchanting and mesmerizing. It's as if they have some secret message in their flashing that makes me feel, "I must have them for myself." So I reach for a mayonnaise jar.

It is said that Japanese farmers tied bags of them around their ankles to harvest rice at night. And people in tropical countries evidently put them in bottles to use as lanterns.

Whatever wooing capacity they have, those *pyropyga* let their little lights shine. They are ergonomically designed and spend themselves with abandon. One hundred percent of the firefly's light is given off as actual light. A light bulb gives off 10 percent of its energy as light while 90 percent is wasted as heat. The fliers glow, disturbing the darkness near them. One firefly can't light up a yard. But hundreds—now that's a light show to be watched.

I think feeling "shine-ish" has little to do with their decision to light up. It is what they were designed for, and they do it.

Last night we finished studying the book of Matthew in our Bible study group, which is really just a ragtag group of disenchanted church goers trying to carve out the truth again from a fresh perspective. But the last part of the last chapter speaks about our call to go and tell. It is called the "Great Commission," and it is the mission-izing of our faith. It is the call to shine. It is what we are designed for.

I squirm a bit.

I have memories of youth group outings to the airport in which we were each given "quotas" of tracts to hand out, fulfilling a loose definition of the Commission. By the bus ride home, we had succeeded in disturbing many strangers and emptying our pockets of brackish cartoon tracts in which people discover the horror that they've been "left behind" and will now face burning in the lake of fire for eternity.

"Turn or burn" reads a local church marquee. "His pain, your gain" says a T-shirt picturing blood pouring down the Savior's face. A silver emblem on the trunk of a Ford pictures the Icthus fish eating the Darwin fish.

Somehow it feels as though this tract-distributing, sandwich-board-wearing, sloganizing, hit-and-run "witnessing" is only 10 percent of the energy behind the light we are supposed to be shining. The other 90 percent is burned off in self-consumed living.

To sum up the Great Commission in those type of "tactics" is to reduce the light of Christ to a clever set of marketing gimmicks and techniques. Kevin Spacey's character in the film, *The Big Kahuna* (whom I don't 100 percent sympathize with, but maybe instead float somewhere between 40 and 60 percent) challenges a young, fresh-faced Baptist employee to explain why his attempts to control and steer a conversation with a potential customer to things of Christ, is any less of a sales pitch than Spacey's desire to sell machine lubricants to the man. In the ugliness of a faceless hotel hospitality suite, the question hangs in the air like mud.

Somewhere between hit and run, and manipulative sales pitching is a call for us to "Let our light shine out of darkness." Whether we feel shine-ish or not. We are called to it.

It is what we were designed to do.

But it has to look more like light shining from our hearts than "gotcha last" soul tag. I'm not saying that tract distributing and slogan wearing are wrong, but they can be destructive if that is all we consider our mission to be. The authenticity of lived faith should be coupled with words that speak light into dark corners.

St. Francis had his own version of the Great Commission: "Go into all the world and preach the gospel. Use words if necessary." This is a powerful challenge. Being careful not to fall into the potential for the permissive laziness of that approach, it is true that no words can undo the testimony that hypocritical living screams out. Saying and doing should not be different. Scripture says it makes God vomit. On the other hand, a life of faith, lived in front of others, speaks beyond words to the heart. *Logos* is essential. In the beginning was the Word. That is where our message begins. But *logos* without *pathos* is incomplete. Let us remember, as we consider the Great Commission, that the *Word* became *flesh*. When we enflesh the gospel, we bring powerful *pathos* to ready hearts.

We should bind ourselves around the ankles of those who can't see, to help light their path. The light in our hearts should shine brightly enough to be a lantern in the dark. All the energy that is Christ should be spent in our lives as a blazing torch to the faithfulness of a God who wants to be in relationship with people. We should become lost in other-centered living. This can be expressed in the uniqueness of who God made each of us to be. Some ballet, some ballroom, some disco.

Use tracts if necessary.

9

Between Safe Places

~

I have no fear of heights. I've been parasailing and hot-air ballooning and would sky dive, except I promised Jim I wouldn't—if he wouldn't ride motorcycles.

I also have no fear of water. I've been amphibious since I could walk. I love the peaceful and insulating quality of being in water.

But while I'm not afraid of heights or water, bridges reduce me to a quivering mess. Perhaps it has something to do with the concept of all that concrete suspended in the air. And the fact that if one were to fall off that concrete at such a height, the water below might as well be concrete too.

I've had dreams about bridges I've never seen before. In my mind they are cantilevered over the water, extending forever into the sky. I'm riding on the back of a bicycle going down an incline that looks like a ski jump, and I miss the last opportunity to exit before the bridge. I am panic stricken. In my dream the same scene repeats again and again.

My gag reflex is becoming overactive just thinking about it.

There is a bridge in Savannah, Georgia, that is a beautifully balanced piece of art. It looks as though it is hanging by thousands of threads suspended from the clouds. We stayed in a hotel that was at the last exit before the bridge, and I nearly clawed Jim's arm reminding him to exit every time we went back to our hotel room. It's quite possible my nightmare was conceived there.

The Cooper River Bridge in Charleston goes up at such a steep angle that you have no guarantee you will go back down until you are already committed to the bridge and halfway across it. I crossed it against my will every few days when we lived there.

The Huey P. Long Bridge in Louisiana is an engineering mistake. It has no beauty and certainly is not ergonomic. Someone started building it before they had thought the thing through. It is unnaturally high and has exactly enough room for two lanes each way. When you are in a van, you sit up even higher, and take up more of the less-than-enough space allotted for each vehicle. It's like trying to cram my size 8 foot into a size 6 shoe. We crossed the Huey P. Long in our van at rush hour, and I had the opportunity to sit on the bridge for an extended period of panic.

Bridges do get you from here to there, from one safe place to another. So if I want to go *there*, I have to use the bridge. And I know, I know, they are perfectly safe. But I still feel the need to cry, drool, faint, or consider alternate routes.

And just so we're clear, nothing is important enough to make me cross the 17-mile-long Chesapeake Bay Bridge/ Tunnel. Nothing.

On the West Coast, the really big dog in the kennel of bridges has to be the Golden Gate Bridge. Its 887,000 tons of concrete, steel, and cable span just under two miles at the Pacific Ocean's entrance into San Francisco Bay. I viewed the bay on that bridge from the back of a 1958 pink Chevrolet Brookwood station wagon when I was four. I sat facing the rear, watching where we had been instead of where we were going. From a four-year-old's perspective, it felt as if I was riding on a cloud, and fear sprouted root.

It's funny how you can blow something out of proportion in your memory. I remembered that bridge as being mammoth. It is big, but only ranks seventh in the category of "largest suspension bridge in the world." When I was 14, I saw it again from the deck of a ship, cruising 220 feet under the bridge. I've seen it from the air, the water, the land, and even been on it. But in my memory, it remained unconquerable. I imagined it as miles long and above the clouds.

The Golden Gate Bridge was the vision of Joseph B. Strauss. He rallied the people, the money, and the politics to build this sky crossing. This Art Deco-influenced edifice opened to traffic in 1938 and was quickly selected as one of the Seven Wonders of the Modern World by the American Society of Civil Engineers. Its 80,000 miles of wire are suspended from two towers that are 191 feet taller than the Washington Monument, and it is foundationally seated 110 feet below the ocean. The bridge was built to withstand 100-mile-per-hour winds coming in off the Pacific and to be able to swing 27 feet from side to side in the wind.

I never want to find out, from personal experience, if this is true.

But with all the brilliant planning and engineering, and the millions of safe crossings, when we landed in San Francisco this summer my legs were wobbly in anticipation of driving over the Golden Gate again. I am a bright woman with a college education, but I was whimpering and cowering like an idiot. I hadn't seen the monster in dozens of years, and it seemed that no logical reasoning would trump my irrational phobia. I tried to ready myself to face my giant. I prayed and was prayed for. I set my jaw in determination and trusted that the rest of my body would follow.

We traveled down Route 1 through the Presidio and Golden Gate Park and at each curve my stomach reintroduced itself to my throat. It seemed as though we would never get to the bridge and then, the next thing I knew, we were almost halfway across it.

I was so caught up in the view that I had forgotten to be afraid.

In the view of the bridge itself I only saw frail wires and unnatural, gravity-defying concrete. The water below was not inviting or comforting, but forbidding and consuming. But when I switched from the view *of* the bridge to the view *from* the bridge, my fear retreated as I was filled with awe at the spectacular beauty.

It was an epiphanic day, and it was the view that slew the giant.

Before me was transparent blue sky and bay, and I gazed at unearthly views of Saucelito, downtown San Francisco, Treasure Island, Alcatraz, and Oakland.

The uncertain passage became a collection of sacred moments. And these moments carried me to the next safe place.

My fear of crossing bridges is not limited to just concrete ones...I deal with emotional bridges as well. Bridges of aging, process, and growth. The view of the bridges fills me with irrational fear, and my heart suggests that I retreat to a familiar safe place. But bridges are the facilitators for progress. They span the distance between here and there—between safe places—and it ends up being a matter of how badly I want to get *there*, to see movement in my journey.

I think the secret is in the choice of view. Is it *of* or *from?* The view *of* the bridge is intimidating and daunting. The view *from* the bridge is incomparable. It's a view that can only be seen from that vantage point of midway through the crossing. Likewise, the view from the passages in life is one that can't be avoided if we are to arrive at the next safe place. It is the view that we can see when our fears surrender to the sacredness of the moment.

It is the view from the bridge.

10

Between Despair and Hope

~

y friend carried their fifth child to term, only to deliver a breathless baby. Nine months of growing and nurturing and becoming, gone now. Her body doesn't know it has no child to feed, so her hormones and breasts and uterus all react to the birth in the normal way. She is continually reminded of what should have been.

A few months later, these same friends found out that their seven-year-old daughter had heart problems that would require surgery. And in the father's words, "the best surgeon on the planet is still just some guy cracking open your daughter's chest." How do you watch your innocent child have a broken heart?

Between these two traumas, their family pet was killed. A local coyote pack was too much for their little fur-ball pup.

So what do I know about despair? I am sometimes moody, fight the blues, and struggle with seasonal allergies. But I love and am loved by my husband. My bills are paid, my family is healthy. There are no coyotes in Hillsboro Village. But I do come to the end of myself often, and then I despair.

Tremper Longman says that "despair looks at the world and notes its emptiness—the lack of true relational intimacy, the utter blackness of death. It concludes that life is not worth it." Despair is the bottom. It is the absence of desire and even the lack of desire to hope.

He goes on to say that the smaller disappointments in life, the "paper cuts, bumps and bruises sting for a while and then go away." But the deep artery-gushing wounds of loss—broken dreams, betrayal, failure, and abandonment—these leave scars that even time won't hide.

I suppose that despair is relative. What is a crushing blow for one is a mere sideswipe to another. But all our hearts are malleable and vulnerable to this beast in one way or another.

Sometimes we don't even know we're in the deep end of despair until we get a crick in our neck from having to look up from the bottom all the time. And sometimes that bottom can be made relatively comfortable, and safe, and familiar. The fear of hoping again, only to be disappointed *again*, is a weight on our backs that keeps us from raising ourselves up out of the slumped over safety of despair.

It's like the proverb that says "even a fool is thought to be wise when he is silent." There is some wisdom in that, but it can become an enabling paradigm for the despairing: *Even the hopeless can avoid despair if they never desire.*

Before we go off into greeting card cliches ("It is better to have loved and lost than never to have loved at all..."), let me put it differently: *Buck up little miss, the safety of shutdown desire is an illusion.* It is a slow death. You've heard the one about the frog in the slow-boil pot?

First of all, the inescapable fact of life is that we are going to face inconsolable sadness. I know this doesn't fit with some Christians' expectation of ease and comfort. We tend to like our Christianity to be neat and tidy, not stained with tears and reality.

Perhaps the young Christians in China who are fired from their jobs for their public confession of Christ could share with us about inconsolable sadness. And the young mothers there who are forced to abort their second, third, fourth, and following children. They would probably struggle with our glib understanding of "the abundant life," our bumper-sticker religion.

But despite our happy religious slogans and pat answers, we will face despair that cannot be mended with a Band-Aid. It will take deep subcutaneous sutures to mend the despair our hearts will sometimes know.

"Is your love declared in the grave, your faithfulness in Destruction? Are your wonders known in the place of darkness, or your righteous deeds in the land of oblivion? I cry to you for help, O LORD; in the morning my prayer comes before you. Why, O LORD, do you reject me and hide your face from me?"

This may sound like the lament of a Greek tragedy, a Shakespearean sorrow, or an English poet. But they are the words of Heman the Ezrahite in Psalm 88. They capture the ache of despair and the cry of agony. They are the words that match the face in Edvard Munch's soul-baring painting "The Scream." It is the expanded form of every heart's eventual shriek, "Help me."

And it is included in the holy Scripture because God is not afraid of our despair.

Feeling isolated some days, I pull the curtains around my bed and put earplugs in my ears so I don't hear or see more than I already do in my head. I borrow from the shadows of good days and sleep through today. And sometimes what I dream when I sleep is better than what I dream when I am awake. Then the sting of disappointment shocks me back into the reality of the moment, and I negotiate with my heart about the odds of risking hope.

Why does the dissolution of some close friends' marriage make me need a nap? And sudden cold winds from a close friend put me in a glazed condition? Why do hints of my parents' mortality leave me in a heap beside my closet? Or responsibilities beyond my threshold make me cry? It makes me want to belligerently shake my fist at heaven and yell, "God, be God and fix all of this!"

In His most despairing moment, hanging on the cross to heal my despair, the Savior cried out, "My God, why have you forsaken me?"

My knots are all undone when I think of the Son of heaven in a despair deeper than that of all the collective broken souls in all of history.

But for the joy set before Him, He endured the despair of humanity, and the abandonment by God the Father.

Moments later, just before blood and water poured from His side, He announced, "Tetelestai!" ("It is finished!"). Not in a weak, defeated voice, but in the resounding boom of thunder crashing through the universe, swallowing death and spitting it out.

Let the napping wake up. Let the hopeless take the risk of hoping. Let the lonely feel the embrace of heaven, and those at the bottom rise up with the flap of their wings.

The Savior has carried our most terminal souls and despairing hearts over the threshold of death and then resuscitated our lifeless beings with the kiss of hope. The hope of heaven, and the hope of now.

Earthly hope is tentative at best. It takes place in the realm where moth and rust destroy. But God wants us to hope, to desire, to dream. To want a good marriage and supportive friends and a restful home are all healthy desires. But we must remember that moth and rust *will* destroy, and that it is the promise of redemption that is our ultimate hope. Redemption begins in the here, but is completed in the not yet seen. And it is faith that hopes in the not yet seen.

11

Between
Want and Wholeness

~

In 1888, a pool was uncovered in northeast Jeru-
salem during the restoration of the church of Saint
Anne. On the wall was a faded fresco showing an
angel "troubling" the water. This was the pool of Bethesda. In
the fifth chapter of his Gospel, John the apostle describes it as
a pool where the infirmed, those in want of strength in body
or soul, would wait on one of five porticoes, or covered
porches. It was said that at certain times, the water was stirred
by an angel and the first one into the pool was made whole.

During a Jewish feast season in the first century A.D., a lot
of people were surrounding the pool when Jesus came up to
one of the waiting men, a man who had been infirm for 38
years.

Jesus knows how long we sit in our infirmities. He knows to the minute.

Jesus asked the man if he wanted to be made whole. At last, after 38 years of sitting and waiting, here was his moment. The answer to this man's deepest longing was standing in front of him. But interestingly, instead of a simple "yes," he went on and on about why he couldn't get to the pool when the water was stirred. His eyes were set on the pool as the source for his wellness. He had been sitting there so long, he had begun to trust in the tradition—the water—rather than the One who stirred it.

The man's longing had died with all the years of waiting and disappointment. Jesus had to ask the question, "Do you want to be made whole?" in order to rekindle the longing within the man's soul.

Jesus the Truth always trumps tradition and superstition.

I am just like that man. It amazes me how often my eyes are set on all the traditionally recognized sources for wholeness, when the Savior of my heart is standing before me offering *true* wholeness.

Tradition required that the man make his own way into the water. Similarly, the law requires of us what Christ does not. It is not by scrambling into the pool by our own efforts that heals us, it is by Christ's invitation, paid for by His efforts. Christ asked the man to do the one thing he couldn't do on his own. Get up and walk. Christ spoke life and wholeness into the settled acquiescence of a paralyzed heart and body.

At your bidding, Master, my immobilized heart is moved.

In this story, Jesus gives the man three instructions. Get up, take up your bed, and walk. Act on your longings, don't plan to go back, and keep moving. G. Campbell Morgan said that Jesus gave him these directions "in order to make no provision for a relapse." There would be no going back. Likewise, He tells us to burn the bridges to the immobilizing infirmities in our lives. And to move on, with our eyes on Him. There is no promise that He will carry us. We are going to have to walk, making good use of our wellness in contrast to the years of no movement. Walking means forward movement, spiritual growth, in close proximity to Christ. But by—and at—His bidding.

I live in Nashville. And I'll freely admit, I moved here with my bathing suit on. I sat by the pool for ten years. I was convinced that my wholeness would be found in the traditional source for singer/songwriters—a record deal. What a lovely and enticing pool. My eyes became so set on that as the source for completing me that I began to lose sight of why I wanted that wholeness to begin with. And to protect myself from disappointments that occurred over and over, I started to bury the longing. The longing that had been planted in me by the Author and Perfecter of my soul. The longing to love Christ and express that in a creative medium. It was what I was designed to do, but the doing can never exceed the being.

My eyes were set on a cheap substitute for wholeness. It wasn't that my longings were too intense, it was that they were not intense enough. I believed I would be satisfied with the healing touch of a record deal, when deeper within me, Christ was calling me to a greater wholeness in Him.

This may all sound a little vague, but I tell you that when my eyes were finally adjusted to a redeemed focus, I saw how small the pool was that I had fixated on in comparison to the Living Waterfall that was calling out to the deepest part of my soul.

It wasn't that the pool, or a record deal, was wrong. It's just that it wasn't the source of my wholeness. Healing, and creative outlets, are not wholeness.

What pool do you sit beside? Have you lost the God-given longings He has placed in your soul? What traditions and forgeries have you set your eyes on that keep you from seeing your wholeness in the Savior's eyes? Have you given up hope and slumped into a settled acquiescence? Do you have a lot of excuses for why you aren't whole?

Do you want to be made whole?

"Get up, take up your bed, and walk."

12

Between
Ho and Hum

❧

isturb me, God. Challenge my complacent comfort. Stir me. Shake me from my ambivalence.
Storm on me, if necessary. But don't allow me to
sit unmoved by life in Your Presence.

Our days filled with status quo and resignation lead us to
a "whatever" attitude toward life and threaten to choke any
remnants of wonder from our existence. Too often, our souls
breathe in "ho" and exhale "hum" to the rhythm of a mediocre
life.

C. S. Lewis captures this condition in an appropriate word
picture. He says that we are all content to make mud pies in
the backyard when we could be enjoying a day at the beach.
The depth of experience and intimacy offered by Christ is

trivialized by our indiscriminate satisfaction with a bumper sticker faith. Our hands are muddy.

We have dipped our toes into the waters of faith, but kept a safe distance from the demands and responsibilities of deeper waters. We just keep our lives moving. As long as we are controlling things satisfactorily, our spiritual needs are reduced to a simple good night prayer with fingers crossed. "God," we pray, "don't woo me to the deep end." Our Bible study is reduced to a dose of chicken soup or a precious moment. And the only time we are really pouring our soul out in the throne room is when we have turned it into an emergency room.

Our sins have been downgraded to "oops" and "oh well" as opposed to being shalom breakers that separate us from fellowship with God. Thus, we feel no need for a sacrificial Savior, just a good pal who puts the amen on all of our plans. Our casual low-maintenance integration of Christ into our schedules is like a cheap surface coat of paint that peels after a few rains. Then the rawness of our lives is exposed to the elements, and we run for a quick patch-me-up prayer and go on our way.

We wonder, after years of this practice, why our souls are leaking and our faith is failing. Unmoved to cultivate the richness of a spiritual life, we have lived a polite, shallow faith, and now find that we are unprepared for the depths of sorrow, anger, betrayal, and disappointment we sometimes face. We live numb lives.

There was once a man who lived a numb life, though not by choice. Because of the undeniably contagious nature of his incurable leprosy, he had to live separate from everyone else. Some lepers even wore bells to warn people of their coming, and held cups on the end of long poles so that people could put food or money in them without ever having to come close to the diseased person. His was a life of isolation and exclusion.

This man didn't know the comfort of physical contact. He watched life from the outside. There were no hand-shakes of introduction and no goodbye hugs. No one brushed the hair out of his eyes. He didn't share the joy of camaraderie and celebrate a victory with teammates, walking with arms around each other's shoulders. His own mother couldn't hold him, and no wife would have him. And even if someone were to touch him, the flesh-eating leprosy had destroyed his nerve endings to the point of making the man numb.

And then... he met the Savior.

The first thing this Savior did was reach out His hand and touch the leper. The thing that no one else could do for him. Jesus broke the spell of isolation and numbness with an unrestrained embrace. The Greek word used for what Jesus did is a *hearty* embrace, not a glancing, casual, careful touch. Jesus pulled the man to Himself. And then He forgave his sins.

From the numbness and isolation of leprosy to the touch of grace, this man would never be the same. Christ asked him not to tell anyone, but how could he not? If you suffered from an incurable terminal disease, and had been numb all your life, then Someone came along and healed you, how could you keep quiet? How could you stoically go on with life, unaffected by the supernatural interruption of your hopeless condition? Why would you choose to return to a numb existence when you had felt the Savior's touch?

We were afflicted with a terminal disease called sin. It ate away at the flesh of our hearts and caused us to be numb. But the God of the universe interrupted time, sending Christ to do what no one else could do for us. He touched us, tore through the walls of our numb heart, and pulled us to Himself. And He forgave our sins.

How, then, can we sit between ho and hum?

How can we not be stirred beyond a comfortable and complacent Christian existence to an explosive love of Christ that leads us to the deeper grounds of holiness? An insatiable hunger and thirst for righteousness? A faith that is moved to action by the sight of suffering, that finds hope in eternal perspective, that begs God to reveal Himself in Scripture, prayer, and experience? A faith that causes the sinews and fibers of our bodies to strain forward in sacred attention to the revelation of heaven in the ordinary moment? And a faith that leads us into the throne room for the single purpose of celebrating God?

How could we ever return to the numbness of mediocrity when we have been touched by the mystery of heaven? The familiar intoxicant of apathy is a wildly addictive drug. Freed of it once, we must be freed of it again and again, daily renouncing it in favor of intentional growth. We must confess our addiction and establish new heart habits.

And pray, "Stir me, O God."

13

Between the
Rain and the Ocean

~

*F*irst it rains. Then puddles collect. Then puddles spill into each other and make ponds. Ponds collect rain and make lakes. Lakes leak into creeks, creeks leak into streams, streams become full and make rivers, rivers rush into oceans.

And that is life.

You are born. You have a mother and father. Then, sometimes, siblings. Then friends, extended family, in-laws, children, their friends and family, the guy at the dry cleaners, the teller at the bank, the cashier, the neighbors, the church, the office, the county, city, state, country, continent, world.

Self magazine, *People* magazine, *Life* magazine. Me, others, everyone.

I am a drop in the vast ocean of humanity. When you look at the ocean, a collective heap of drops, it looks dark and unsearchable. But when you hold one drop in your hand, it is transparent and knowable. One drop is significant but not personally distinguishable from another except through the lens of an instrument designed to know them one by one.

I suppose if I started off as a drop of rain in a storm that fell into a creek that flowed into the Ruvyironza River in Burundi and traced the Rwanda-Tanzania and Uganda-Tanzania borders into Lake Victoria, and then passed by the now-flooded Ripon Falls into the Victoria Nile and followed it northwest for about 300 miles through Lake Kyoga, and then raced over the rocky rapids until entering Lake Albert, I could leave out the northern end of the lake into the Albert Nile through northern Uganda and into Sudan where it becomes the Bahr al Jabal. I would slow down a bit in the swampy south of central Sudan through As Sudd, which is the accepted dividing line of the Arab-dominated regions in the north and the African regions in the south. Then the river becomes the White Nile, which joins the Blue Nile in Khartoum. Northeast of here, the Atbarah is the last tributary to feed the river, and the Nile takes an S-shaped turn through the Nubian Desert. Six waterfalls later near Cairo, the longest river in the world spills into the Mediterranean Sea. Passing through rain forests, mountains, savannas, swamps, and deserts, it covers 4,160 miles.

I would have quite a history as a drop in the Mediterranean. Although they all blend into a homogeneous collection of water, every drop from the Nile would have a different history. Some would be bruised from the rapids and rocks, others would be windswept from the falls. Some joined the river in Khartoum, others in Sudan. It would be their specific stories that distinguish them from one another in the context of the sea.

How is it that God can name every drop in every ocean? Probably He knew them or someone in their family before they started their descent from the heavens and collected in bodies of water below.

It feels as though I've been through most of the experiences of that drop in the Nile in my life in one way or another. I've experienced rocks, waterfalls, deserts, swamps, and the temporary anonymity of lakes. I've hit patches of stagnation and had to be disturbed by wind and weather to keep moving. The specific details of those passages distinguish me from every other drop in the ocean. And when the eyes of God (which are designed to know us one by one) are turned on me, He knows me.

And I so want to be known. Sometimes lost in the immensity of life, a little voice in me blurts out, "know me."

Do You know my voice, and the doubt behind my smile? Do You know the uncertain feet that pursue You? Do You know the curve of my neck and the smell of my hair from the other billion dots on this planet? Have You heard me speak Your name?

Is it You that disturbs me when I get complacent and stagnant? Do You call me to deeper waters? By name?

14

Between the
Aisle and the Window

~

We made our reservations for Albuquerque weeks ago, so I am visibly unhappy when the skycap suggests that we should "hurry on down to the gate" if we wanted to get seats together. I stomped my right foot on the ground as my eyes rolled back in my head, and I sighed audibly. This tactful response, of course, coaxes a less than gentle heaving of our suitcases onto the luggage cart. We'll probably lose our worldly belongings to the purgatory of the Atlanta airport.

Jim takes off in a jog for the gate while I deliver our van to the satellite parking lot and ride the cold, soulless shuttle back to the terminal. Why do we have to call it a "terminal"? Is that really a good name for the last thing I see as I am catapulted into the air in a 40-ton hunk of metal?

I stare with envy in my heart at the other travelers on the shuttle, thinking they probably have wonderful aisle seats in the exit row on all of their respective flights. When the bus reaches the terminal, I gather myself and lower my head, prepared to body slam anyone standing between me and good seats. After being stopped at security and having to remove nearly everything but my metallic green nail polish, I proceed to the faraway wilderness to which United Airlines gates have been banished. I finally see Jim walking towards me with "we got bad seats" body language. Not only would we not be sitting together, we would each be serving four-hour sentences in middle-seat hell.

I am a tall, but small, person, and large flying people take advantage of that. They spill their bulk over my armrest and spread their hulking shoulders into my personal area, borrowing air from what little space I have secured for myself. In the middle seat, I am simply consumed. I cross my arms at the elbows and try to balance my bobbing head in the center of the headrest only to discover later that I fell asleep and drooled on the navy blue shoulder beneath my mouth. As I am dressed in a white shirt and the window-seat person is in a snappy chartreuse number, it is safe to assume I have gotten closer than I intended to the aisle-seat person.

Comfort aside, there are distinct middle-seat responsibilities as well. The passing of food and drinks and passing back trash are assumed functions. Chatting up the fliers on your right and left is also assumed. I make a move for relational isolation by pulling on my lavender-scented black satin mask and stuffing bright yellow earplugs in my exposed princess-pink ears.

Ontologically speaking, as a middle-seat dweller, I live and breathe as a flier, but enjoy neither a spectacular view nor freedom of movement. I have none of the privileges of a window-seat dweller, observing breathtaking sunsets and glimpses of earth and having the support of the side of the plane to sleep against once the view digresses to the tops of clouds. Nor do I enjoy the privileges of aisle space and easy in-and-out access of my seat. In fact, the aisle-seat person is the control contact for the whole row. They control the flow of snacks, blankets, pillows, and bathroom passage. No, I have none of those privileges. I am a middle-seat person. I am in between.

I do not have by nature a middle-seat personality. My husband is a middle child, the middle-older of four. He sees all sides of things and is able to be friends with anyone he meets. He is a peacemaker and a fixer. He has the skills to navigate the middle-seat world. But I am the youngest of two by nine years. That makes me the baby. I see my side of things. I am the princess. The one who gets her way. The window or aisle person.

I must come earlier next time.

Goldilocks was a middle-seat woman, without all the crankiness. She actually found it to be just right in the middle seat. And I suppose a small attitude adjustment could help me to become more comfortable with my situation. In the middle seat, you don't have the draft you get in the window seat sometimes. And you don't have to worry about a cart coming down the aisle and whacking your elbow the way you do when you sit in the aisle seat. And you certainly won't be left out of any enchanting conversations that take place in your row.

It's beginning to sound pretty good, isn't it? Perhaps you'd be willing to trade seats with me then...

Actually, there was Someone who took my place in the middle seat. Someone who accepted the middle seat with humility and willingness. He saw the middle seat as a place to bridge the extremes of heaven and earth. To be the one mediator between God and humanity. He surrendered the privileges of Godness in heaven to clothe Himself in a servant's skin. Not viewing His Godness as a thing to be grasped or clung to, He surrendered it willingly, knowing it would ultimately cost Him His sinless life.

On the middle cross.

Between two guilty thieves, He strikes up a conversation. With each of them. The thief on His left and on His right. And before "it is finished," one thief acknowledges his own depravity and is headed to paradise with Him. After their last breaths.

For God so loved us, He sent His Son to become the middle-seat person.

15

Between the Tare and the Wheat

~

I don't plant weeds in my garden. I'm not a horti-
culturist, but I am an intentional planner. I carefully
select what I'm going to plant after browsing
through numerous catalogs and magazines. Interestingly,
you'll find little to no advertising for weed sales. So if no one
is selling them or planting them, where are all the weeds
coming from?

The first year I lived in this house, I planted my garden
in the backyard. Careful planning and my innate obsessive-
ness found me hacking away with a hoe in the early spring.
But even after the neurotic care I gave my plot, unwanted
things still invaded the soil. In spontaneous spots, inside and
outside of the garden, green pointed things began to sprout.
I hadn't planted them, and they weren't part of the plan, so
I took my gardening shears and cut them off at the dirt.

They came back the next year.

By then, I was a bit more seasoned as a gardener. I even
had my very own gloves and trowel. So I approached the

plot with a bit more authority and dug up the bulbs that were causing my problem. I suppose it just takes a little experience to learn how to deal with these things.

The next year, they were back again. And they brought friends.

There evidently were bulbs that didn't sprout the year before and had enjoyed more room since I'd removed the others. They were multiplying faster than I could keep up with. So I had to go back and do *more* surgery. Carefully, I carved and separated the unwanted plants, trying not to disturb the roots of the good plants.

I troweled with precision. I knew that if I didn't keep up with their self-propagating tendencies, they'd take over the garden. So I had to keep risking the health of the flowers by digging up the weeds.

I didn't plant the undesirables. But the person who lived here before did. And I bear the consequences for her bad choices.

My soul is soil. And the Spirit toils it until it is fertile and ready. Then the Father plants in it. I receive the seed of faith, and surrender my life to Christ.

The salvation seed is planted, and when it takes root, it is more than perennial, it is eternal. The Spirit continues to fertilize in expectation of fruit.

The salvation plant is not in danger from weeds once it has taken root, but the yield of fruit and blooms can be. Love is growing well. Joy is a seasonal bloom that needs special fertilizer to maintain its growth. Peace is a quiet bloomer at the base of all the other plants. Kindness and goodness and gentleness thrive next to love, and faithfulness is a steady grower. But patience is challenged by the weed of restlessness, and self-control is most often choked by the weed of personal-rights. These weeds were planted by the person who used to live here, and I bear the consequences for her bad choices.

The weeds *must* be pulled, but they are often deceptively lovely. In the early stages, the weeds mimic the intentional plants. It's sometimes not until the bloom, or fruit stage, that they can be distinguished.

In some of the first recorded parables, Jesus tells of the Planter, the good seed, the bad seed, and the field. (See Matthew 13:24-29.) The Planter scatters the wheat and the enemy scatters tares. As the wheat begins to grow, the weeds do too. The workers were concerned, but the Planter said that when the wheat matures, you can recognize it from the weeds and safely separate the two.

There is a weed that grows stealthily among wheat. It is called the bearded darnel, and it looks identical to the wheat—until they are both ripe. The fruit of the wheat is heavier than the bearded darnel, so heavy, in fact, that it causes the plant to bow when it is ripe. The bearded darnel stands stiff-necked.

Whatever does not bow before the Father, is a weed.

The sin nature I inherited allowed the enemy—the one formerly in control of my life, to plant weeds. In contrast, when I surrender my life to Christ each day, He continues to plant the fruit of the Spirit in me and dig up the weeds.

Sometimes I nourish weeds in my soul-soil. In the early stages, they can be passed off as good. But when the fruit doesn't bow, the ruse is over. The healthy fruit of patience will bow, but the fruit of restlessness will not. The fruit of self-control will bow, the fruit of personal-rights stands stiff-necked.

The hand of God is sure and deftly wields the trowel in my life, separating the fruit from the weed, the tare from the wheat, that at the name of Jesus, every knee would bow.

When the peonies in my garden bloom, and their full flowers arch to the ground, I am reminded.

16

Between Ebenezers

~

*W*hen I was a kid, I kept souvenir remembrances. According to my romantic memory, I saved them in an old cigar box, so I call them "cigar-box memories." I think the truth was that I stuffed them all in a Barbie lunch box. But a cigar box is so much more like Scout in *To Kill a Mockingbird*. So much more literary.

Whichever kind of box it was, it was meant for the safekeeping of an unlikely group of apparently worthless items. But if the pieces could talk, they could tell stories. They are reminders of how I got from one place in life to the next.

I saved things like the button from a favorite blouse I'd outgrown, a symbol of time's relentless passage and untamability. Four-leaf clovers I'd found went in the box. Fragile and dry, reminders of the unexpected, they floated between the layers of treasure. Money my dad brought back to me from foreign countries (which felt heavier than ours) gave a dull jingle to the box. The coins told stories in my head of the mysterious places my dad had gone and linked me to persons I would never know. I pirated the spoils of my sister's perfume, symbols of the girl/woman I would always be. Empty bottles of Shalimar or White Shoulders became bounty for my treasure box. The smell of my sister, consequently, was all over my collection of memories.

Sometimes I would sit on the floor beside my bed and empty the box, taking inventory on each souvenir of my life up to that point. I remembered. Usually it was with contentment, but occasionally it was with the sigh of lessons learned. A failed Popsicle tree planting, for example, resulted in my digging up the Popsicle stick "seed" and placing it in my box. A reminder of my early botanical experiments.

As I got older, the box bulged with photos, letters, broken jewelry, and memoir-like notes. An old set of Dad's cuff links, near-empty lipstick tubes from Mom, and eventually a graduation tassel. Tokens, icons, keepsakes, reminders. Holding the cuff link reminded me of my dad in his dress-blue uniform, handsome and smelling of Old Spice, ever the guardian of my security. A purple ribbon from VBS (Vacation Bible School) was a symbol of achievement in spiritual discipline and Scripture memory. A charm waiting for a bracelet yoked me with my mother and her sisters, reminding me I am not alone, but connected by heritage.

My method of storage has changed several times over the years, but the selective saving goes on. Gifts of covenant between my husband and me are stored in a jewelry box. So are a dried rose and a dried carnation. Both pink. Both from my grandmothers' funerals.

In the entrance of our home is a small birdbath holding rocks. I decided they were wonderfully organic reminders of places and moments. I have a rock from Addison's Walk, where C. S. Lewis walked and meditated on the grounds of Magdalene College. I feel more tangibly aware of him and his insightful faith for having it. I have rocks from a restful and restoring weekend on Whidbey Island. Rocks from Paris, London, Austria, and the homes of my family members. They are solid and lasting; sure, unyielding to weather or surroundings. And they remind me.

One of the problems with living in between is that we forget to take the faithfulness of God with us. We forget, as the psalmist says, the "wonders" He has done. Caught up in the uncertainty of what's next, we tangle ourselves in the skein of forgetful faith.

If we are to live in the sacred now, we will need reminders. Some souvenirs of grace. Something reminding us of God's consistent care for us, some Ebenezers.

The Israelites started a sort of rock collection in Mizpah. (See 1 Samuel 7:1-13.) They had been in battle with the Philistines. Their hearts had wandered and they had forgotten Jehovah. Their God-box, the Ark of the Covenant, had been stolen by the enemy. And they thought the magic of deliverance was in the box. But when the Ark was returned, they found they were no better off than before. They were still under Philistine oppression.

It was not the presence of the box, but the condition of their hearts that invited deliverance. Until the rivals for their affection were renounced, until all idols were destroyed, they would not be restored. They finally understood and repented at a place called Mizpah, throwing away their idols in a sign of submission to God, pouring out their hearts before Him in fasting and prayer. And that day the Lord delivered them from the hands of the Philistines.

So Samuel built a memorial from a large stone at Mizpah to symbolize God's care and provision. A reminder of Jehovah-jireh, past, present, and future provider. They named the stone "Ebenezer," meaning "stone of help." Whenever they or future generations passed by it, they remembered.

What stones shall I collect? What will remind me of God's faithfulness to deliver? Because as the hymn writer wrote, I too am "prone to wander" as the Israelites did. So I also need an Ebenezer to remind me, that "hither by Thy help I'm come."

17

Between the Windows

~

The humidity finally fell below the 36 degrees north latitude mark last night on its way dripping south to the equator and friendlier places. I hated it. My friends all hated it, so did the dogs and babies. Even the cats joined in on this issue. Too humid. So we willed it gone, and it is leaving. The heat is unpleasant enough, but the humidity that sends the bead of sweat down my lower spine is just plain bad. I'm a writer. I know these things.

We've been outside soaking up the unpleasantness while cleaning our windows this past week. I don't think cleaning them once in 11 years makes us look like obsessive home-owners, but I don't do a completely thorough job on two of them in the front, just so people won't talk.

How did anyone do this before the invention of squeegees? What a great tool. I want to use one on my mirrors and bathroom tiles and possibly my face. To protect my delicate digits, I've been wearing orange rubber gloves during the entire project, and the humidity has created a greenhouse effect inside the gloves so that I have to take them off and dry my hands every few windows.

I should mention that 12 of the windows on our cottage-home have storm windows with 13 screws in each of them. That's 156 unscrews and 156 screw back-ins. But aside from eight mosquito bites and three abrasions from the ladder, I'm coping.

Did I mention that the squeegee is a foolproof tool? I've mixed up my own cleaner with water, a couple of drops of liquid dish soap, and a dash of vinegar. Spritz the liquid on the glass, drag squeegee over it, wipe squeegee blade with towel, repeat. Stunning effect.

So I do all the inside windows, then the outside windows, and begin to see dramatic improvement. An easy 40 percent more light in the kitchen. But once we take down the storm windows and have access to the glass that was in between, things really take off. The windows become so transparent that I'm afraid the dogs will try and jump through them.

On some of them, the storm windows have protected the interior glass, and it isn't much work to clean. Just a quick swipe or two and it's done. On others, I find trapped slime water that leaked through the caulking, creating some unknown scum on the windows or giving safe harbor to spiders and their webs. But everything must go.

Without access to those interior window panels, I'm afraid we would have had a breakdown in our cleaning enthusiasm. But getting in between the windows was like cracking the last of a code and satisfying the driving need to conquer.

On the door to the screened-in porch, there is an insulating type of glass. Two panels of glass with a vacuum of air between. This keeps the temperature sealed in or out, which is great. Except that someone at the factory forgot to clean the glass in between before they sealed it all up. So now I have less than perfect vision of my porch through those doors, and they bring the grading curve down for the whole house.

Access is everything in the cleansing process. Sometimes storm windows are extra layers protecting the innards from exposure to harsh weather. Sometimes they are unknowing partners in sealing in corrosion and unwanted guests.

My interiors have storm windows and storm doors and insulating glass. One by one the screws and barriers must be removed to allow access to the hidden places. The Cleaner is done once He can see His face reflected back in the glass.

I don't know if we would have completed the project if the humidity hadn't left. The truth is that there are still five storm windows waiting to be put back up. I'm sure we'll get to it before the cold slams in. But for now, I'm airing out the innards.

18

Between
Here and There

⁓

Trapeze artists swing back and forth to build up momentum, finally letting go of one bar as kinetic energy sends them off into the unknown. I mean, they know they are headed for the next bar, but between here and there it's a blind leap of faith that carries them through some very serious unknown.

They are instrument flying.

A few years ago I was coming home from the funeral for my dad's mom. I was somber, and it was hard to leave. Add to that, I was booked on a four-seater "paper" airplane that flies between Hyannis and Boston. It was me and the pilot and my bag. We were the last flight they allowed out that morning because the notorious Cape Cod fog had begun to consume the air. The pilot had made the trip hundreds of times, but you tend to think of it as his first when it's your first. As we rose into the curtain of air, I strained to see anything in the grayness ahead of us.

When we were up a few thousand feet, the perky pilot turned around in his seat to face me and started up a conversation. I answered with quick one-word answers, hoping he would turn around and pay more attention to where we were going. Finally I blurted out a bit of concern, and he calmly explained to me that he didn't need to see where we were going because we were flying according to the instruments.

I thought about the last few years of my grandmother's life and how most of her memories had disappeared into the fog of Alzheimer's. She left this world through that fog, holding hands with Jesus, to head full speed into the known and yet unknown. Instrument flying.

Everyday I get up and sit at my computer and stare into another empty document that needs to collect an assemblage of characters that will form words, sentences, and thoughts. I start with a vague idea of where I'm going, but mostly it is also instrument flying. I type one word and then another word and hope that that sentence will lead me to the next one. It is familiar but always as scary as the first time. You have to attack it full steam and trust that you will get where you are going. And if you don't, you will pick up and start again tomorrow until you get there.

Anne Truitt says this is like the run the horse rider must make. The creative writer, painter, sculptor, (mother, father, professional, dreamer, planner, husband, wife, friend, pastor, plumber, doctor, etc.) gallops into the night in the driving rain catapulting themselves fully into some direction. When, on occasion, it is discovered that it is the wrong direction, the rider might stop and while regrouping, may enjoy the company of friends and peel the mud off their feet for a bit. But "in the back of their minds, they never forget that the dark driving run is theirs to make again."

Balancing the input of experience and intuition with the knowable factors of empirical data, we daily put one foot after the other, flying by the instruments. Instrument flying has a destination which can only be glimpsed by flying on through to the other side of the fog. It is sending a child off to college, moving from one place to another, losing a family member or friend to death, taking on a new job, leaving an old job, starting school again after raising a family, trading in the rat race for a fishing pole or watercolor brush, leaving singleness for marriage, childhood for adulthood, day for night, and doubt for faith. It is a call from the past to the future, from what was to what is yet to be. Sometimes it is a call away from the familiar, but to something more desirable in the end. But to be sure, instrument flying can be quite exhilarating.

Noah was an instrument flier. He built a very large boat. He was faithful to the call of God on his life even when the fog was thick and it was difficult to see where he was headed or why he was even doing what he was doing. Everyday when he faced another piece of cypress that had to be planed and wedged into place on his incomparable task, I'll bet he wondered if he was riding full speed in the correct direction. But everyday he got up and made his dark run, with an eye to the sky watching for clouds. Eventually, it rained. And he needed his boat.

Moses flew by instrument. Inexperienced travel guide that he was, he gathered up God's people and led them away from a threatening past into the promise of a future. Trusting his instruments, Moses came to know the provision of God on a daily basis. With the vision of promise as his distant goal, for 40 years he got up every morning to throw himself full speed into his wilderness fog.

Martin Luther King, Blaise Pascal, Benjamin Franklin, Michelangelo, William Wilberforce, Dietrich Bonhoeffer, the young virgin named Mary who was pregnant with the Son of God, Paul the apostle, the disciples after the resurrection. All were courageous instrument fliers. Daring the unknown, they flew to the other side of the fog, trusting not in their own senses but in the faith that had sustained them so many times before.

Flying by instruments is what walking in the Spirit is all about. I surrender my own intuitions and senses to something I cannot see. That surrender is called faith. Dallas Willard says, "Faith is not opposed to knowledge, it is opposed to sight." So when I walk, ride, or fly into the fog, I trust the instruments, because my senses will mislead me.

I can't see the next page I will write. Or how I will get through the fog of midlife to the other side, whatever is over there. But I know that if I will fly by faith and not by sight, I will land in the right place. I know that as a promise better than I know it by practice. I can't help thinking that if I could just see a little bit more clearly, I'd be better at this. But then, that's not faith. And it seems that faith is the best way to travel between here and there. Between this trapeze bar and the next.

19

Between
Earth and Heaven

~

Tonight I received the news that my cousin finally gave up her battle with cancer and left her frail body to go home. As her eyes and heart are filled with heaven, mine are filled with tears and memories. She was good. She was a strong woman who endured more than what seemed her fair share, and she completed her journey before we were ready to lose her.

The end feels so final. She won't answer the phone when I call or chortle over life's ironies with me. Her unborn grandchildren will not know her smell as she snuggles them to her neck. And she will not grieve her own parents' death. The place she occupied on earth will be retired with the scent of her breath on it.

Death is a thief, grief is a bully, and loss is a bruise that only fades with time.

There is cause to weep. Jesus wept when His precious friend Lazarus died. Some people think He cried because of the sorrow He felt for those left behind, Mary and Martha particularly. Others think He cried simply because of the loss of Lazarus. I think He cried because everything around Him whispered, "The wages of sin is death."

From the first time the heart of God was broken, a salty tear fell from heaven to earth. Sin was "the vandalism of shalom" as Cornelius Plantinga has said. He quotes Athanasius, who wrote that because of that first sin, when God's command was spurned, we who were made from nothing became "bereft of being" and began to physically disintegrate. Death was invited into the garden. And that was not the way it was supposed to be.

The disintegration of our body and soul was not in the initial plan. Lazarus was never intended for death. My cousin was never supposed to die. Neither were my grandparents, my uncles, my aunts, my older baby brother, and every other living creature since the beginning of time. That was not in the Designer's heart for His creation.

But God is a loving Father who allowed us to choose death, and then sacrificed His Son to purchase life back for us.

The salty tear from heaven that fell in the garden was a promise of preservation. Jesus' tears at Lazarus' tomb were an amen and an omen of what was to come. God the Son would preserve the creation by the spilling of His own blood to buy back life.

I am 41. When I was five, my mother's father died. I ate graham crackers and milk and wore my hair in a loosely collected ribboned ponytail that my dad prepared for me while mom was gone for the funeral.

I still just want to eat graham crackers and let my father's able hands brush and gather my hair and reassure me that my world is fine.

But I ate the last of the crackers sitting on the screened-in porch while reading on this humid Sunday afternoon, unaware that Gail was struggling between earth and heaven.

I am a full grown woman. My father and mother live a plane ride away.

My husband sleeps beside me, his breathing normal, rhythmic, and reassuring. So I untie the ribbon in my hair, roll over next to him, and surrender to another loss from my telephone/address book.

But not without hope. Gail's name has been written in a new book. The Book of Life.

20

Between Meals

~

"No snacking between meals." Are they serious? They're not the boss of me.

Right now I'm eating nuts and drinking a canned Coke. And I feel good about myself. I ate a sub sandwich for lunch, but I want a snack now. Sometimes I'll have two Vienna fingers and a cup of herbal tea. On rare occasions, I'll have half a bag of Oreos and a bottle of water. But frankly, I eat meals so I can have snacks.

Those people who say "no snacks" need to loosen their ponytails and start wearing comfortable shoes. I mean, even in kindergarten we had snack time. If it was so horrible, do you really think they'd teach it to us in our beginner years?

Ok. I agree. We were never *promised* snacks. They were usually motivators for good behavior. They are not "givens," but privileges. And if we don't eat our meals, we get no snacks. Because then they just aren't good for us.

When Jim and I take driving trips, I eat nothing but snacks. I know it's bad, but...I start in the morning with white donuts. Midmorning some Twizzlers. Lunch, a fast food restaurant. Afternoon, cheese puffs and a Coke. Dinner, pizza. Late night snack, Mylanta.

When you eat nothing but garbage, a couple of things happen to you. First, you feel like a hot air balloon, and second, you get grumpy and tired. Seems there's no real nutritional value in that stuff. So your engines run down and your systems get depleted.

So eat good meals, if you're planning to snack. That's probably what they meant to say.

In my spiritual life, I find that I snack more than I should. Surviving on fast food prayers and half-page devotionals leaves me spiritually malnourished. And then I wonder why I feel overwhelmed and unsure of the future. It's because I have little spiritual sustenance on which to draw. I need to refuel.

Taming my craving for snack foods means retraining my taste buds for things of nutritional value.

The Israelites who wandered in the arid wilderness were hungry. But they were hungry for what *they* wanted. God provided daily bread for them. Manna. Miraculous falling-from-heaven provision. But it was hard to taste the sweetness of heaven when they longed for the savory food they had eaten in Egypt.

St. John of the Cross puts it like this. "We long for our own wretched food, and are nauseated by the indescribable blessings of Heaven."

I hunger for Egyptian cuisine (my way) when daily bread (His way) is the taste I need to develop. But it is a taste that can only be developed through quiet and discipline. God's mysterious manna is so much more nourishing than the empty calories I settle for.

God desires to feed us and meet our needs. He is the bread of life, who offers Himself to us as daily bread.

At the end of His life, Jesus fed the 12 in a small upper room. In a symbolic gesture of what was to come, He broke the bread and poured the wine, His body and blood, the provision for our sins.

Some days, I need the quiet and solitude of intimate prayer, of one-on-one presence. On other days a fully physical engagement with my garden and the fruit of the Creator's hands satisfies my spirit's needs. Sometimes I am filled by the corporate experience of worship with other believers. At other times sitting alone in the pew of an empty cathedral fills me full of awareness of God's transcendence and faithfulness.

These are all good things, but only if I am feeding on the Bread of Life. They are supplements to the daily requirements. To read the Word of God and meditate on His story and its application to my life provides nourishment and sustenance. To see the tradition and history of people of faith from Genesis through the Prophets, the Poets, the Gospels, the Epistles, and into the book of Revelation; watching them struggle "back then" the way I do now, feeds my heart. To be reminded of the unending faithfulness of God to generation after generation builds spiritual muscle on my lean frame.

And between meals, I enjoy the company of friends, an inspirational movie, and some favorite authors. Healthy snacks.

I was praying the Lord's Prayer nightly for a season, and as I meditated on the picture of what daily bread looks like for me, I wrote out a little acronym.

B: belief, beauty, because, benefits.

R: rest, redemption, righteousness.

E: epiphany, Eucharist, energy.

A: assurance, affirmation, application.

D: delight, desire, direction, deliverance.

And as I prayed, "Give us this day, our daily bread..." these began to take shape as realities in my life.

I started putting on some weight. The good kind.

21

Between the Storm and "Peace Be Still"

~

In April 1958, when my sister was nine years old, she met with a sudden storm. Older sisters rarely have a say in whether or not they get a baby sister. These little packages, whose cries permeate the walls and disturb the quiet of an only child's world, demand constant attention, threatening the sovereignty of the older child's kingdom. Just when my sister's world seemed manageable and secure, I entered. The new baby girl. All the attention and time and affection that had gone to her was instantly cut in half. Her stock had gone down.

Christmas, birthdays, surprises, rides on uncles' backs, special times at the park with Dad, girl time with Mom. All of it was previously her domain, but now she had to share it with a mussy-haired, fat-cheeked, toothless little drooler who couldn't even talk. I know I would have put up some resistance. But not my sister. She had a gracious and generous heart from the first time she heard of my impending arrival.

From the day I came home from the hospital she embraced me as her little sister. I'm pretty sure the incident where she dropped me on my head when I was nine months old had nothing to do with sibling rivalry. But ever since, I have milked it for whatever it was worth.

Nine years difference in our age set us up to have a good chance at liking each other. There wasn't much opportunity for competition. But the beauty, talent, and style of an older sister had its natural affect on me. I was enchanted with her. I wanted to dress like her and wear my hair like her. I remember the orange and green towels we bought for her dorm room when she went to college. I thought, "Someday I'll have nice towels like these."

When I was three, I had a four-foot-tall baby doll. When Mom and Dad went out for dinner one night, sister Melani dressed me in the doll's clothes and fixed my hair and makeup like the doll's too. When our parents arrived home and Mom saw me sitting and talking on the couch, the doll incarnate, she nearly expired.

Melani and I went to carnivals and movies and parks and out for ice cream. We were girlfriends. We sat up late on weekend nights and watched scary movies in her bedroom until I couldn't hold my eyes open anymore. I wore her hand-me-down clothes and bikini bathing suit, even though there were, as yet, no "developments" to hold it on. Every Christmas she gave me a special nightgown that I'd get to open Christmas Eve and sleep in. She taught me to sing and love art and poetry and scream for the Beatles.

When she graduated from high school, my father was in the navy, stationed in Viet Nam. Times were tense. She fought for her own voice and was challenged from all sides. Faced with choices and experiences common to most young adults in the sixties, she carried scars and regrets for a lot of years. But at her graduation, on a sticky day in Memphis, Tennessee, I was proud to be her little sister, and felt a certain responsibility to fill in the hole that Dad's absence left.

I guess they were seating people with children in the back of the gymnasium auditorium so we wouldn't be disruptive. But I was ticked. I couldn't see from back there. They ought to let the short humans sit up front and the tall ones in the back, I reasoned. We were certainly capable of good behavior for the length of the ceremony. But as no one else had evidently thought of that, I was in the next to the last row of folding chairs on the paper-covered gym floor. They droned on and on through the A's, B's, C, D, E, F, G, H, etc., etc., etc. Our last name was Wright. I'd be able to take a short nap and still be back in time for the W's. But as they rounded the T's and the W's were in sight, I slipped out of my chair and slid into the middle of the aisle in the back of the gym. The view was unobstructed and when they announced her name and handed her her diploma, I hopped and drew my hands up under my face and squeaked, "That's my big sister!"

The next few years were lonely ones. Melani was off to college. Even though Dad was home from Viet Nam, and we had moved to Virginia (just outside of D.C.) into a neighborhood plump with children my age, there was a hole the size of a big sister in my heart.

We stayed as close as possible through occasional visits and phone calls. She even moved back home for a while before she met and married her husband. She gave me right of first refusal on him. If I didn't like him, he was out. I voted yes and harbored a secret crush on him until I found my own.

In February 1976, I was faced with a sudden storm. I had been to youth group that Sunday night and when my boyfriend (now husband) brought me home, we could tell by the slump of Mom's shoulders and the "I have to be strong" look on Dad's face that something was wrong. They had received a phone call that Melani had been in a car accident, and it didn't look good. She was alone in the car, so my baby niece and brother-in-law were fine.

It seems that a van had run a stop sign on a road that crossed a highway between Bryan and Brenham, Texas, smashing into the driver's side of the Volkswagen bug my sister was driving. There was no glass left in the car. The driver's side door had been ripped off and the driver's seat spun 90 degrees, taking the brunt of the hit. The steering wheel was torn in two and my sister was tossed like a rag doll.

We flew out on the next flight from Washington National to Houston Intercontinental Airport, rented a car, and my mom, dad, and I drove the 90 miles to Bryan-College Station in anxious silence.

And the winds and rains crashed around us, and the thunder cracked and the lightning split. And we cried, as the disciples had done in Mark 4:38, "Lord, don't you care that we perish?"

When we walked into the hospital, we didn't know whether or not she would be alive. The surgeons had stepped away from the table three times, giving up. They had emptied a garbage can of blood from her limp body, had removed her spleen and three feet of her intestines, patched her other insides as best as they could, put a pin in her leg, and rolled her into the ICU to struggle between life and death. They were waiting for a helicopter delivery of her rare blood type when we got there. The doctors had transfused her eight quarts and were out of it in the hospital, so they had put out a plea for more on television and radio.

I couldn't help. While it was the same familial blood that rolled through our veins, I carried O-positive, hers was Rh-negative.

A couple of hours turned into 6, then 24. Then the crucial 36 and 48, and it looked as though she would make it.

A month later, she was out of ICU and in a regular room. It would take a few more months of mending before she would be sent home. I reluctantly returned to Virginia to finish out my senior year of high school.

In June of that year, I walked across a stage on the football field of Jeb Stuart High school to receive my diploma. And I looked out to see my sister, standing in the front row with the aid of crutches, hopping and squeaking out, "That's my little sister!"

Peace be still.

22

Between Naps

~

*W*hy is it that if the phone rings and wakes us from sleeping, if the other person at the other end of the line says, "I'm sorry, did I wake you?" we always quickly answer, "Oh no, of course not"? The reason, of course, is that we worry that we'll somehow be perceived as lazy if we are still sleeping or taking a nap.

Before we were five, our mothers begged us to be sleepy and take naps. We were praised and rewarded with cookies and milk after taking a long nap.

I want this practice reinstated.

There is way too much shame associated with rest in our culture. Busyness is the altar at which we pour out our priceless selves. The busier we are, the more pious we feel about how busy we are. We wear our to-do lists like proud medals telling the world that "Hey, I'm important because I have a lot of things to do!"

Have you ever heard a conversation like this: "Yeah, I got up this morning, read for a while, then took a walk. I came home and made some lunch and took a wonderful nap. Spent the afternoon reading and dozing on the porch and then made some dinner. Afterwards, I ran a hot bath and soaked with some good music for a while and then hit the bed early. It was a very productive day." Other person: "Wow, you got so much accomplished. I don't know how you do it all." Hmm.

Rest is an essential we too often deny ourselves. I recognize that not everyone actually has a schedule that would allow for a day like the one I described, but the truth is that even imagining a day like that causes most people to feel guilt and shame for not wanting to be more productive.

There is a reason why everyone I talk to usually mentions how tired they are within the first few sentences of a conversation. Men, women, old, young, parents, nonparents, single, married—everyone is tired.

We are all screaming internally that we are exhausted. We'd very much love to take naps, but we can't because we've lost perspective on what is truly productive and valuable in our day. Where is the bravery in working ourselves into a frazzled mess? When did napping become shameful and overcommitted lifestyles become something to applaud? We assume importance and diligence on the part of those driven beyond their safe boundaries, and accuse nappers of being lazy and unfocused.

We have devalued wellness. It's ok to go to a doctor when you are sick, but we see taking vitamins, eating well, exercising, and getting enough rest as almost fanatical. Insurance companies only cover prescriptive health care, not preventive. Better to stress ourselves all the way to the gas station, running on fumes, than to take the time to refill when you're still a quarter of a tank up. Better to end the day cranky and exhausted, having accomplished everything on our lists, than to have napped and completed less "stuff" so that we are more than just a shell of a human being at the end of the day.

In the last year, I have become a dedicated napper. The truth is, one of the few things I am totally committed to on a daily basis is napping. I have taken to the belief that napping is part of my work. I sense the naysayers snickering. For me, it is a necessary item on my to-do list if I am to be a whole person with anything to offer others in words or actions. In some ways, life is just the stuff that goes on between naps in my world. And frankly, I deal much better with that stuff if I am faithful to my napping commitment.

Aside from the physiological benefits of good rest, the mental dividends are unmatched. Whether it's 20 minutes or 2 hours, when you wake up, your brain is on the edge of its seat, in the ready position. There is a distinct benefit to rebooting your mind in the afternoon. Things that were beginning to clog the mental highway get shutdown and must once again find an orderly route to the front of your consciousness.

And even aside from these benefits, there is a repositioning that takes place in our souls. We once again are reminded that we are the creature rather than the Creator, when we surrender to our need to nap. Alister McGrath has said, "The tiredness that is so important a feature of life on the road of faith is something that we must acknowledge, along with our own inability to cope with it. Yet in His grace and love God is able to renew us and enable us to continue the journey in hope." When we rest, we are recognizing His strength in our weakness. We discover our need for the refreshment that only God offers. Isaiah unashamedly said that we will mount up with wings as eagles, because God gives strength to the weary. Are you weary? Jesus said, "I will give you rest." There is no shame in accepting this offer.

In the afternoon, I put on napping clothes. Those are clothes that I don't mind wrinkling and that won't restrict my sleeping movements. I take off my earrings and my watch, both of which are stumbling blocks to good napping. I carefully fluff my bed and luxuriate in the down pillows supporting my head. Anxious thoughts are filed under "I promise to think about that when I wake up." I put on my eye mask and surrender myself to the unseen Arms that safely hold me through my rest. I enter the shadows depleted, and wake restored.

The sleep tonic lubricates my dry soul.

Between naps, I work hard. Fully charged, I fully spend myself. I'm pretty driven, but if I neglect my naps, my work—not to mention my attitude—borders on sludge. So if you were to call me in the afternoon, I might be napping, and I would proudly answer the phone, "Yes, I was asleep."

But you'll have to take my word on that, because now I'm going to unplug my phone so I can nap, uninterrupted.

23

Between Titles

~

For the last 20 some years, your title has been "Mom," but today your last child left for college. Old toys packed up, trophies and ribbons and photos saved, and then quietly, childhood surrenders to the inevitable. Now who are you?

As the wife in a marriage, your title has been "Mrs." One half of a team, the second signature on the mortgage. But he's gone. Now who are you?

The title on your desk and on your door read "Vice-President." Everyone came to you for advice and for approval. They told you today that they will no longer be needing your services and asked for your keys. Now who are you?

You've always been first in the local marathon. The blue ribbons collect by your desk. You casually put them in the open wooden box each year, confident someone will see and congratulate you. It feels good to be "Number One." In this year's marathon, someone bettered you and crossed the line first. Now who are you?

She always called you her "best friend." You were the one she turned to and counted on. Someone new is in town, and now she's turning to her. The best friend seat at the table is taken when you walk up. Now who are you?

You've always been confident about how you look. "Good looking," in fact. You took care of yourself and watched your diet and could count on your body to respond well. But now, you see your sizes climbing and your muscles failing. When you walk into a room, heads don't turn your way the way they used to, but towards the younger, firmer bodies. Now who are you?

You were the best: champion, queen, king, captain, and a million other titles until something changed that. The labels of description that covered your heart are stripped back to reveal simply a person, only distinct from the rest of the crowd by the uniqueness of your fingerprints. And now you wonder who you are and if anyone cares.

But a resounding Voice from heaven answers "You are mine."

The One who created you, who formed you says, "Do not fear. I have redeemed you, called you by name, and given you a title, 'Mine'"

Isaiah 43 informs us of the consequences of being "His." When you go through the high waters, He is with you. The rivers won't sweep you away. When you walk through fire, you won't be burned. Because the Holy One of Israel, the Savior, finds you precious.

Tape this promise to your door, your mirror, your forehead. Your heart. It is enough.

24

Between Rains

~

Their tiny white five-petaled heads, each with a pink period in the center, struggle to stand tall. The ceramic-green leaves have begun to curl page-boy style. It is hard enough to live isolated in a garden pot, with limited resources for complex root systems, but it has also been an unusually dry season. With the normal weather conditions, the potted vincas that bookend my front steps thrive and give the illusion of botanical genius living behind the front door. Not now.

Even the grass has gone beyond angry. The fist shaking and whining that goes on when thirst first sets in takes too much energy now. The chlorophyll-less threads remind me of my husband's Grandma Pearl's delicate thin hair. I consider purchasing a baby brush and brushing the patches. Under one tree in the back yard, there is still some lovely jungle-green grass. It preens like a preteen girl unaware of her youth and firmness in the company of her mother. The mother struggles between the pride she takes in her offspring and her anger at the ravages of gravity and time. The green, tree-shaded grass has no idea of its good fortune. It is not sympathetic to the dying collection of grass around it, but probably would be if it knew that even in the shady comfort of the hackberry, as time goes on, the heat will consume it as well. Its thick green blades will become thin pale threads.

Deep fissures of water-worn paths have split the ground, and the earth's dermis is exposed. This is the dry and thirsty land where there is no water. Where David's soul thirsted and his flesh yearned for God. And my heart is also split and my interior exposed. I am as thirsty as my front yard, and as hard.

When I turn on the sprinkler (which is a poor substitute for rain because it is just two tiny outstretched three-inch metal arms with pin holes in the ends), the water seems to turn to steam before it lands on the ground. Can steam nourish grass? It is water in its essence, but in this form can it impart thirst-quenching elements to brittle, fallow ground?

I have tried to water my heart with steam. I know that I am restless, and so I call a friend to discuss my "issues." She is Christ en-fleshed for me, so I delicately peel back the layers and expose the dermis of my interior. My friend is faithful. She listens with empathy and "hmms" and "oohs." These are the two words my sister told me to insert in my vocabulary when what I mean is "I'm sorry for your problems, I'm glad they aren't mine, and I really don't want to know any more."

I hang up the phone, temporarily moisturized.

But before I can set my mind to become productive at something, the moisture has evaporated, never reaching below the surface.

I am between spiritual rains. It is not so much that I am expecting the flooding of "event spirituality" to quench me, but I find it difficult to survive on mere daily fidelities. For a season, I was moving along, well lubricated in the joys of gospel readings and the psalmists' laments. Then I followed a formal daily devotional book that gave me a healthy diet of Old and New Testament readings, along with prayers, hymns, and meditations from various deep-thinking authors. And it was enough. Until that day when once again my prayers lie flat in the back of my throat. My tongue is fat and my heart is disconnected from the spiritual umbilical cord. And no matter what I do or say, my soul is in a dry and weary land, where there is no water.

I am experiencing what the sensitive St. John of the Cross referred to as "the dark night of the soul." This phrase speaks of those times when our connection with God seems strained at best. We lack what he calls the "sweetness in the things of God." He distinguishes this time from lukewarmness in that we still have solicitude towards the things of God. We are not complacent, but we feel disconnected. St. John of the Cross suggests that the Lord allows us to experience such times in order to prepare our spirits for a renewing time. And is it not true that were it not for the dryness of the desert, we might not appreciate the rain?

Consider the Israelites. There was no water. They had traveled a long time. Moses and Aaron were good leaders who listened to God and the people. But there was still no water. And the people were still wanting water to wash down the strangely flavored manna, not having yet developed a taste for it. So they whined for water. The miraculous provision of manna from heaven was not enough to assure them of God's care for them.

I would have been frustrated by the complaining of the Israelites, but Moses was forbearing. The people caterwauled about not having any water and how much better it would have been if they had all died. God couldn't help but overhear their melodramatics. They listed their complaints: lack of figs, grapes, pomegranates, grain, and, by the way, THERE'S NO WATER TO DRINK!

The Israelites had stuck God in their own "God-box." They had determined that because there were no lakes, no ponds, no streams, and no rain, therefore there was no water. Surely God could only provide in those expected ways. They put their tiny God in His safe box on the shelf.

When I am in a dry place, I look for provision in my God-box places. I expect Him to be in the predictable places like church and my prayers. But often there is a rock which I need to speak to that will gush forth with His presence. An unexpected step of obedience required to open the flood of refreshment.

God told Moses to speak to the rock, and then water would flow. But it is unnatural to get water from a rock, so Moses had little confidence in God's simple suggestion. He added his own flourish. Instead of simply speaking to the rock, he hit it twice in a dramatic self-gesture. And even through Moses' lack of faith and obedience, God was faithful and sent water. But it cost Moses his entry into the Promised Land.

When I am between rains, do I recognize God's provision? Or do I continue to try and find it my own way? And will I miss the Promised Land because of my insecurities and unwillingness to do what God tells me to do, in the way He says to do it?

During my dry time, I tried to be faithful to the sources for spiritual rain that I knew. Readings, prayer, quiet. But there was no rock that gushed. Not that I spoke to many.

One hot afternoon a few days later, when I walked to the end of my sidewalk to get into my car, I looked down and found three separate four-leaf clovers standing faithfully with the other three leafed clover and the broadleaf and remaining wisps of grass. I know what you are thinking. That is not a voice God used in any Old or New Testament stories. No, it isn't. But then I've never seen a leaking rock either. Luck resulting from the finding of a four-leaf clover is purely sentimental superstition, I know that. But four-leaf clovers are rare. At first glance they appear to fit in, but on closer examination you recognize them as different. They are quiet nonconformists. They are my people. And I love them, so I always look for them. And God knows that, and He used them to remind me that He was walking in my dry everyday-ness with me, and in the midst of brown grass there were not one, not two, but three tiny green-leafed symbols of water to a thirsty soul.

Sometimes God's provision is fierce and sudden and overwhelming. Sometimes it is subtle and quietly reassuring. But in the morning after the dark night of the soul, the things of God are sweetness again. And having come through to the other side, I am confident that I will feel dry and removed again, but for now, I drink until I am more than full, and I slip the four-leaf clovers into the pages of favorite books in case some other dark night, I need a sip of water.

25

Between
Waking and Sleeping

~

I'm deciding between the perfect tanning lotion and the "how-to-make-a-million-bucks-without-doing-a-thing" video. My glow-in-the-dark legs could use some perfect tan, but then, with a million bucks I could buy all the tan I want.

I ruled out the abdominizer thing and the fruit dryer the other night. Too hard to store. And with as little meat as we eat, the make-your-own-sausage gadget, clever as it is, is out too.

So it's $30 for a tan, or three easy payments of $89.50 for a million bucks. I just don't know if I'd take the time...

I have "The Big Eye." My father named it that, and he's bought a few "as seen on TV" items to prove he's been there. It's always between the hours of three and five A.M.

when I can't seem to sleep. I open my eyes just enough to know I'm awake and try to drift back to sleep. But then toss, toss, turn. Toss. I'm awake and there's no going back.

I don't want to read because I really don't have the comprehension skills I need at that time. So I collect my favorite blanket, go quietly to the downstairs den, and lie on the couch with the remote in my hand. One time the battery in the remote was dead, and it took me until four o'clock just to scrounge up a couple of functioning double As from the starlit kitchen.

There is absolutely nothing of any substance or entertainment value on TV at that hour. I know this is a revelation. In general, it's sales pitches and news anchors who don't have the hair for prime time. So I watch and pretend to buy things. I write down one-eight-hundred numbers and decide to call on the magic mops, spot removers, mandolin slicers, hairdinis, aerators, and mulchers tomorrow, when I'm near my credit card.

I'm usually ok with this middle-of-the-night festival of awakeness as long as I can get back to sleep before the sun makes an appearance on the horizon. Once the sun comes up, it's over. I must get up. I've missed my chance for things like dreams and snoring and things normal people do between night and morning.

It was in this same night/morning twilight that an adolescent Jewish boy named Samuel couldn't sleep. Before the sunrise, a voice had called him three times. He was unfamiliar with the Father's voice and mistook it for Eli's, his master. Eli, the priest, though old and filled with regrets, finally identified it as the voice of God calling Samuel. He directed him to go back to bed and when he heard the Voice again, to answer, "Speak, LORD, for your servant is listening" (1 Samuel 3:9).

I'm not trying to say that every time I can't sleep, it's God calling me. I might have come to the conclusion that I was fairly important by now if that was the case. Sometimes it's just too much caffeine or not enough exercise or unreasonable amounts of stress that keeps me up. But I have to believe that sometimes, in the quiet unique to that twilight time, when my own voice and the other noises in my life are silenced, the Voice of heaven who knows my name might want to converse with me.

And so I pray. Usually I start with every member of my family. If I finish with them without becoming distracted by the actual "what" I'm praying for, I move on to my friends and acquaintances. Then there's the country, the world, hunger, peace, etc., etc. By then I'm usually getting more stressed about all of the things I'm praying about, so I try to think of things I'm thankful for to induce some peace. I go through the alphabet from A to Z and think of something for every letter. Then I'm pretty much completely awake, and I reach for the remote.

I missed the point.

Eli told Samuel to go back to bed and when he heard the Voice again to say, "Yes, Lord, I'm listening." He didn't tell him to go back to bed and pray for the entire string of humanity. He told him to acknowledge the voice of God, and listen.

We're uncomfortable with the silence. If there isn't going to be an actual audible voice, we often feel obligated to fill up the quiet. Let's face it, still small voices speak best in quiet times. And while I can't say that I've had a lot of times where I might have thought that maybe I really heard a Voice, I stand no chance of hearing if I'm going to fill every opportunity with noise and busyness and the stuff a good strong din is made of.

So one by one I try to silence the noises of my heart.

Training my heart to silence and my ears to heaven is not easy. One of the Desert Fathers said that preventing distracting thoughts from coming into your head is like trying to catch the wind in your garments. It can't be done. Our job is to say no to them when they come.

Kathleen Norris tells of trying to teach about silence to a fifth-grade class. One of the students said the silence was scary. "It's like we're waiting for something..."

We are.

We are waiting for the unfamiliar voice of God to speak. Because He owns heaven and earth and dispenses suns and stars at His pleasure, we expect a dramatic and booming voice that will cut through our personal noise. How arrogant to think God would use His King-of-the-Universe voice just to speak to us. Surely we are significant enough for something more than a still small voice. I know I've certainly used my If-I-Were-King-of-the-Universe voice to reach His heavenly ears from time to time. "HELLO GOD, HELLOOOO. I BESEECHEST THINE EAR, INCLINETH TO MINE VOICE..." Testing, testing, is this thing on?

We fill up the silence because we are afraid He won't. And there we'll be awake, alone with the God of the universe and the sound of crickets.

But He does fill up the silence. Sometimes with the sound of His indescribable presence, which isn't always very loud in my ears. But it communicates louder than thunder. Sometimes it is a mild impression or sense of peace or a distinct feeling. On rare occasions, it is a voice.

And sometimes, the quiet Presence brings an untroubled sleep.

26

Between
"Dear Lord" and "Amen"

~

ometimes prayer feels like the sound of my own voice, echoing off the walls of heaven.

For now, the walls of my heaven are painted acacia green, in a semigloss. And the echo is loud enough to stir my schnauzers in the other room to come and poke their tar-black noses into my office to see who I'm talking to. "Who" takes up more spiritual space than physical, so they are satisfied to return to their silent watching in the other room. On their leaving, the Father blinks at me as if to say "continue," and I find I am still stuck somewhere between "Dear Lord" and "amen."

Rilke says that ever since our becoming and then falling, we have stammered fragments of His ancient name. But I invoke it with the anticipation of His faithful response.

It is a shattered image of God that we reflect, and the fracture lines of sin make tracing His outline an effort just beyond our reach. We see dimly now. Until we see face to face, we wrap ourselves in Christ and approach the throne room.

I grew up in the American evangelical school of prayer. "Are there any prayers or praises tonight?" And for the next few minutes broken arms, aching backs, colds, flus, and cancers were brought to the Father. Traveling mercies and momentary brilliance for taking school tests were requested. Souls of unbelieving friends and family were submitted for Holy Spirit wooing. Finances and football teams were blessed. I kept a red notebook full of prayer requests with various levels of check marks beside them as answers came. Or wishes were granted. Or to-do lists were done.

Somewhere between "Dear Lord" and "amen" we went shopping, so to speak. "I need one healing, two blessings, one forgive me, and an even dozen protect me's, please." In the simplicity of this approach I suppose I did relieve my anxiousness, but I'm not so sure that I encountered the presence of God. Ever the productive American, I checked off the box beside "prayer" and moved on without sitting still long enough for the scent of heaven to fill my nostrils.

Missionary Rosalind Rinker spoke of the importance of listening to God rather than just making "prayer speeches" at Him. I'm not discounting the fact that we are invited to "let our requests be made known." It just seems that if we spent a little more time on dwelling in the presence of the God of All, our needs list would seem smaller.

It is the paradox of the closeness of "Our Father" against the transcendence of "Who art in heaven" that my husband says sets us up for the mystery of the faith. I mean, "Our

Father" wants to know about the skinned knees and disappointments and requests for traveling mercy. But "Who art in heaven" transforms the trivia of my humble petitions. "Our Father" shows that there is Someone who cares. "Who art in heaven" shows there is Someone who is able. The mystery is the grandness and yet the personalness of prayer. The same hands that cupped the mud and fashioned it into all of humanity, cup the tears I spend in private desperation. How can I be needy when the God of heaven has given me access to His ear? But how can I *not* list my concerns when I have *access to His ear?*

As Dallas Willard has asked, how can we make sense at all of an intimate relationship in which there is no specific conversation? Part of conversation with God is running through our "lists," but the "amen" shouldn't follow immediately. "Dear Lord" has to compel us to our knees in awe and wonder. Because while He is the Father of our cares, to be in the throne room and not feel the heat of the flames on the tips of angel wings, or feel the rhythmic pounding of my heart in tune with creation as if all of time was pregnant with this moment, and not be moved to speak of His wondrous unspeakableness, is to be numb to the presence of God in prayer and surrender the opportunity for intimacy with Him.

And then there is the Son. How can I be in the presence of heaven and not put words to the wonder of God in skin? He became my kind. The Reconciler, who offered His fragile flesh so we could stand before God. He offers the bread we hunger for.

St. Anthony said that prayer isn't perfected until the one praying loses sight of himself or the fact that he is praying.

I suppose it is this work of the Holy Spirit that transports us from self to surrender. From speeches and lists to stirrings that have no words.

I am sure of this, the One who knows my name, knows me by the whispers of my soul, sees my blemishes and acknowledges them, but applauds my will beyond my ability. And some mysterious collection of my lists mixed in with contemplative communion is the response of a faithful heart.

Amen.

27

Between the Filling and the Spilling

~

*W*e have this treasure in earthen vessels, that the surpassing greatness of the power may be of God and not from ourselves; we are afflicted in every way, but not crushed; perplexed, but not despairing; persecuted, but not forsaken; struck down, but not destroyed; always carrying about in the body the dying of Jesus, that the *life* of Jesus also may be manifested in our body." These words are from Paul the Apostle (2 Corinthians 4:7-10 NASB, emphasis added).

But I don't feel like this. I feel inadequate, unable. I don't feel strong, and I definitely think this earthen vessel has some cracks in it.

Just when I think I've begun to contain this mysterious "filling," a circumstantial moment of doubt cracks my resolve and the next thing I know, I'm dripping my treasure out in a trail behind me. One minute I have begun to recognize my adopted status as a daughter of God, the next I begin to doubt my heritage. I understand, but I can't seem to maintain a functioning fullness.

Won't the morning ever come when I get out of bed and once and for all can say, "Lord, I think I've got it now"? I mean, I can go to sleep at night, filled with the reassurance that all of my anxieties have been cast on an able God, and I can rest in the childlike trust that while I may be perplexed, I need not despair. But no more than eight hours later I am awakened by the fact that I am overwhelmed, unable, stressed beyond my coping. I peek tiny, slitted eyes over my comforter and decide I am too depressed to venture past my bed today. Somewhere in the night I spilled my filling.

Most days, somewhere between the filling and the spilling is where I live. God has filled me to the measure with His fullness. Filled me to the measure with enough of His fullness for today, this moment. But when a friend with whom I have vulnerably shared myself, subverts my trust or joy, I spill a little. When my high expectations of a professional opportunity are met with a far lower reality, I spill some. When my husband, family, and friends need more than is left in my emotional-giving account, I spill. When I am grumpy to the point of aiming at neighborhood cats as I drive down my street, I realize I must have developed a slow leak. When I'm afraid about the future well-being of my loved ones, a major artery is hit, and I gush.

I suppose it's a matter of appropriating the treasure that keeps one topped off. Having the fullness of God has to have more purpose than just carrying it around. This spiritual treasure is not a dead-weight-do-nothing-hanger-on type, like a diamond ring or a string of perfect pearls. Those are museum treasures—nice to view, but fairly useless. If I had to, I could tie the pearls around my waist to hold up my pants, but on the whole they basically exist just to be admired. Not that there's anything wrong with that, it's just that the spiritual treasure we are intended to carry around in our vessels is interactive. It is most treasure-able when it is used.

Two days before we were supposed to leave for a trip to Florida to be with the rest of my family for Christmas, we learned what freeze plugs are. They are things in the engine of our van that make it ok to drive to be with family for Christmas in Florida. But they were not well. It seems the van's recent hiatus from road work caused a little cancer-type problem. It is our second vehicle, for jaunts around town, so we don't use it much. It used to be our main form of transportation for out-of-town work. The last van we had we drove 380,000 miles and went through three transmissions. But a year after acquiring this van, we started flying to most of the events where we were speaking or playing music. And while we thought we were being kind to our van by not overworking it, it was actually decaying.

It seems there is this issue with antifreeze and freeze plugs. One needs to drive the van so the helpful blood-like engine coolant can circulate through the chambers of the engine. But because we didn't drive the van, which is the *raison d'etre* of a van anyway, the antifreeze ate through the freeze plugs and the engine could no longer hold its liquid. Tiny little pinprick holes in the freeze plugs allowed water and antifreeze to slowly leak out of the engine. That is what the critical care van doctor told us, and then he told us it would cost a lot of money to repair. I did not want freeze plugs for Christmas.

When you don't drive your van, the treasure inside will eventually leak out. And, by the way, it leaves a stain.

The treasure of Christ inside of me was meant to do more than just sit there. It is the lifeblood of my soul, and when I don't live and move in ways that make use of it, it seems to just leak out. The analogy breaks down, because Christ has promised to never leave us or forsake us. But how full of His Spirit we are and how that is appropriated varies in relationship to our level of surrender at any time.

When I develop a leak, I can use a temporary "stop leak" such as emergency prayer or the strength of my husband's spiritual life or the wisdom of favorite authors. But if I am to appropriate the treasure in a functioning fullness between filling and spilling, it will take an ongoing conversation with the Spirit in which I surrender to His leading. I trade in my eyes for the Spirit's and begin to see life redemptively. When my friend wounds me, I own my culpability, but allow the wounded hand of the Savior to comfort my heart. And I am reminded of the forgiveness shown to me, and my opportunity to show forgiveness, because of the life of Christ in me.

I speak these things because I know they are true, not because I have mastered them. I find I am best at enjoying the treasure when I am alone and unprovoked. But I fear developing a spiritual leak if I don't use what is inside of me. Perhaps that is why I find that I do not live in a world of just me.

28

Between
Giving and Receiving

~

*W*e got a letter today from the parent of a child we sponsor through Compassion International.

"Dear Mr. and Mrs. Thomas,

First of all, let me heartily greet you and concerning us through God's mercy, we're also okay.

Thanks to you who at all times pray for my son's good health. Regarding his studies, it is also fine, now he is already in Grade 2.

I'm glad because every Sunday he attends the Sunday School and he has learned many things about the Lord.

How are you? Hoping you're always in good health and away from harm.

Thanks for your letter and for praying for my son that he will grow up having good health.

He was happy because they went swimming to the river and had a lot of games when there was a

Family Day at the Student Center. By the way, thank you very much for your support to my son because he was able to purchase a bag, school supplies, and clothes.

Until then, thank you very much for helping my son. May God bless you."

I have lost sight of who is the giver and who is the receiver in this relationship.

29

Between
Here and Home

~

I've been gone from home for two weeks now, which is only 14 days longer than I wanted to be gone. But the trip has been good, the time of ministry with students fruitful, the financial rewards notable, and the interaction with some peers and long-distance friends an unexpected pleasure. Yet still, the umbilical cord stretching 800 miles is cumbersome, and I feel the life being sucked out of me.

I have fought my way through to the end of each day, counting down the nights I must sleep in a foreign bed. I wash, brush, floss, rinse, moisturize, and medicate before donning my night blinders and earplugs, preparing to Sominex my way to sleep. Just before shutting the day away, I open my Hildegarde of Bingen book and sob through her words that speak my heart:

> And doubt seizes me, and I say "It is useless."
> And again I want to fly above the clouds,...I
> feel in myself only the unrest of doubt, des-
> peration, sorrow and oppression in all things.
> *But I will not yield to the frail clay;* I will
> wage a furious fight against it.

I lay awake long enough to go a couple of rounds with my clay, and then sleep overtakes me.

Our part finished, we packed up and left the quaint beach lodge, saying goodbye to friends and colaborers in the fields. We arrived two hours early for our flight home. We were only mildly anxious. The Philadelphia airport is nothing if not big, busy, and overwhelming. After having entrusted our worldly possessions to a curbside skycap whose con-versational skills were on the level of a disinterested ado-lescent boy, we proceeded to have our vocabulary tried and tested by the car rental return clerks before boarding the shuttle to the terminal. In each of these encounters, I tried to take on the "how can you use me God, in this moment" attitude that Jim and I are trying to employ. But, of course, not wanting to be "fake," I find myself slipping back into the far more comfortably fitting "me first, too bad about you" attitude I have rehearsed for so many years.

The next five hours found us pacing the terminal along with 2500 other delayed fliers, only to discover that our flight was completely canceled and the next available one was not until 8 A.M. the next morning. I sat in my tear puddle for long enough to satisfy my poor-me need, and then gathered myself together. As we taxied to a nearby hotel with vouchers totaling $23 for dinner for two in a hotel restaurant, I realized there would be no washing, brushing, flossing, rinsing, or moisturizing tonight, as all I had on my person were three books, a laptop, and some ChapStick.

Scraping our pennies together, we were able to eat wilted salad and a glue-like substance they had named cream of potato soup downstairs in the hotel restaurant. One Coke each, add tax and tip, and we only had to dig into our own purse for about $4.25. That doesn't include the $5.00 more for a Sprite, orange soda, and brownie from the vending machine to wash down the glue flavor left in our mouths, but who's counting?

Our 8 A.M. flight the next morning left the gate at 9:30 A.M., and when we finally landed in our hometown, I was dangling by the last nerve in my feminine reserve. I cheerily flagged down the friend who had come to return us to our home, and turned to help Jim with the baggage, when it was made clear that my suitcase had been subjected to its own nuclear holocaust somewhere between Philadelphia and Nashville.

As I stood in line at the customer service baggage desk, I counted the teeth in my mouth with my tongue in order to keep from speaking words of insanity. Finally, I got my credit voucher for a new bag, a pair of pants, and the antique compote that had been mangled inside my suitcase. The bag was so pitiful that the man behind the counter asked if I would put the contents into another bag so that he could have mine, never having seen one quite that destroyed. Posterity. My own personal disaster was posterity for him.

All I wanted was to get home.

I am in transition. I am in between. I am flying the trapeze. Somewhere between out there and home. Jim and

I travel professionally. I've become pretty good at making anyplace a temporary home. I take my own real teacups, special candles, soft clean washcloths, and, of course, incense to make every place smell like home. The first thing I do when I get to a room is nest it. I take any little signs or folders or hotel-ish notices and stuff them into drawers. I rip the bedspreads off of the beds and pull back the blankets so all I see are white sheets. If the chairs are stained and disgusting, I cover them in towels. I stack my books and Jim's books beside our respective sides of the bed. I light the incense, put on room socks and slippers, so as not to touch the floors, and sit still on the bed with as many pillows behind my head as I can fit. I pray God will make this place home for the duration.

But after a while, all my tricks to convince myself I am at home fail me, and I realize I am in nobody's idea of home and I really, really want to be at MY home. I have no ruby slippers, but I still feel a little bit like Dorothy.

How did God the Son handle His long trip away from home? I wonder if He lit "throne room incense" to remind Him of heaven, and if once in a while He put on His heavenly skin to make sure it still fit. Did the sounds of heaven linger in His ears when He tried to pray, and did He sometimes hum a song the angels taught Him to pass the time in the workshop? And just exactly how did He faithfully occupy until His time was complete?

He certainly had a to-do list of sorts. Virgin birth, overachieve in Temple, crash diet in desert with wicked tempter, pick 12 guys to work with—one of whom who would betray Him, spread the news of fellowship with God and forgiveness for sins, revolutionary lifestyle, defend prostitutes against self-righteous religious leaders, dine with drunks and geeks, heal, heal, heal, and suffer the long dark night of the soul before willingly being murdered. All this before He would be able to go back home.

It wasn't as though He didn't ask to be sent home early though. I mean, not all of these things were fun things to do, and you have to believe that the memories of heaven make every other experience on His out-of-town business bland by comparison. So He asked His Father if it would be ok to come home early. And when He wept at the grave of His dear friend Lazarus, I can't help but think He was also home-sick. And when He looked at the works in progress—John and Peter and Andrew and James—I think on occasion He saw them the way they would be when they all got home. And heaven was so visceral and close for Him on the cross that He even took a friend home with Him that day, to Paradise. You only take people home with you when you love home.

I love home. I have asked to go to my home in Nashville early, but the Father has said "occupy, for now." So I begin to make to-do lists for when I am on the road. Love the person in the moment, speak truth to those who are hungry, grow into the woman of God I need to be, and, oh yes, buy more incense.

And then, when He chooses...I can go home too.

30

Between Crime and Punishment

~

J was almost five. The early signs of female obses-
sions were already budding in me.

I had plenty of dolls. A sufficient number to play a game
I called "Orphanage," where I would adopt out my dolls to
imaginary families. Each doll was dressed in its own unique
clothing, some wearing from-the-factory outfits, others a
combination of toilet paper and washcloths. But I'm getting
ahead of myself. Let me back up.

My dad was in the military. The navy demands a man's
loyalty, attention, and, to a large degree, control of his geog-
raphy. For the first 20 years of my life, my father honorably
complied. His presence at Christmas, Thanksgiving, birthdays, and other holidays was never promised. Therefore, for
much of my childhood, my father was held in an icon-like

honor in our home. We mailed care packages full of oranges, chocolates, and pictures to the *Caliente* somewhere in the Pacific, or McMurdo Sound in the South Pole, or Saigon in Viet Nam, or whatever temporary port of call my dad dutifully called home. We anxiously awaited his letters in the daily mail and gathered around one phone for rare ship-to-shore communications. My mother filled my sister and me with stories about our Dad, so I grew up knowing him in the way you know and love a favorite literary character. He was bigger than life; a symbol of the honor and dignity characteristic of the time.

Now before you feel concerned or worry that I suffered from this lifestyle, let me tell you that I didn't. I loved my dad, and I knew he loved me. Meanwhile my mother, sister, and I formed a cement-like bond that has carried me through to adulthood. And now, as an adult, I know my dad in the way that I always wanted to. Up close and personal.

The level of integrity demanded by noble military service spilled over into our home. There was a fairly specific road we were to walk and not much room for deviation. Looking back, I am grateful for the character that this formed in me. At the time, however, I bucked it as often as I could, just to make sure it was real.

So I was almost five. And the girly tendencies shaped in me by God and environment began to show. We lived in one of the high-rise phenomenons of the early 60s. From the fourth floor I surveyed the barren winter landscape in Alexandria, Virginia. There would be no playing at the edge of the woods behind the buildings today. So I would have to entertain myself with inside tasks. Well, I thought, before I could open the "orphanage" for the day, I needed to dress myself and the "children" appropriately. Toilet paper and washcloths would not be enough. I would have to expand my resources to the unlimited coffers of my mother's room.

As I brazenly sneaked into her room to select the needed items, she was cleaning the kitchen, unaware of the crime afoot. Like a squirrel shopping for winter, I gathered some shoes, lipstick, and perfume, then stealthily returned back to my room. As stealthly as an almost five-year-old can. I left a trail as obvious as mud on white carpet. Drawers left open, previously organized shoes left in chaos, and a perfume bottle lid rolling in slow motion to the edge of the dresser I had climbed open drawers to reach. Not to mention the sprinkling of talcum powder I left, having made use of it right there on the spot.

Behind the closed door of my bedroom, I silently reveled in red lips, rather crudely colored as I hadn't even mastered crayon work yet. I sat on the edge of my toy box and crossed my legs to imitate a womanly pose while Mother's spiked high heeled shoes dangled from my toes. And before I opened the "orphanage," I sprayed generous amounts of Chanel No. 5 on myself and each of the babies.

I suppose it was the cloud of expensive perfume traveling down to the kitchen that alerted my mom to the goings-on of her youngest daughter. She graciously knocked on my door and opened it at the same time, catching me red-handed... and lipped... and cheeked. There was no out-of-control outburst of anger. Just a fierce recognition of the situation and a slow, determined gathering of her things, as well as the scariest words a child can hear, "When your father gets home, you will be punished."

I sat on the toy box for a while longer, barefoot, as tears snuck out of my eyes. The rest of the afternoon seemed to last as long as the entire ice age. I pressed my hands flat against the window, feeling the cold outside transverse both glass and flesh to reach bone. And I waited for my father to come home.

Anticipation of punishment is a torture beyond torture. It is perhaps a parent's most powerful weapon. Having to "think about" the crime and its ramifications, imagining what punishment will be doled out, deters future crimes sufficiently for children like myself. Particularly the child of a military man. I would need to shape up.

My poor father, as many fathers of that era, arrived home from work late that afternoon after fighting traffic and professional nonsense, expecting a quiet night with his wife and two daughters, beginning with a warm dinner. Instead, he was assigned the corporal duties of head of the household. I'm sure it troubled him that some of the precious time he was actually home, and not on a ship somewhere in the middle of an ocean, had to be spent correcting me. But loving me as he did, correction had to be delivered.

The only thing I had to say in my defense was that mother and I were *sharing* some of her things. Dad pointed out that I was the only one aware of that arrangement, so we made a deal that I wouldn't "borrow" her things anymore without asking. I cried. And he hugged me. And I was relieved of the guilt my tiny heart could not bear. Punishment, appropriate to the crime, should rightly have been mine. Justice, blind to the face of the criminal, weighs out the perfect balance of crime and punishment. But I received more than punishment. I received grace.

The punishment was bearable, but anticipating it was torture. Sometimes it is in the time between the crime and the punishment that the real price is paid. And when my crimes today are not as marginal as some stolen makeup, it is the time that the Father lets me sit awaiting the consequences that is so unbearable.

I am not speaking of salvific justice here. Nor justification. My crimes were paid for by the sacrificial death of the Son. In this grace I am saved from eternal death. Jesus did not say, "Wait until your Father gets here." But in the space of time and flesh, there are crimes and punishments to be worked through in my daily sanctification. I am grateful that the life of faith is not about what Dallas Willard calls "sin management," but I know that the pollution that my sin causes must still be worked through. When I lie, it does not negate my heavenly reservation, but it breaks the covenant I have with God to be constantly in pursuit of holiness. Punishment shows in broken relationships, loss of trust, loss of integrity. When I lie, there are consequences that grace will get me through, but not without culpability.

Because of Christ, we are no longer slaves to sin, but to righteousness, resulting in sanctification. In other words, when I steal lipstick, I am not sentenced to death, but my wretchedness shows me my need for Christ, and results in my lifelong desire to be more like Him, culminating in heaven.

When Mom was here last month, we went out to lunch one day. After we ate, I pulled out my lipstick to redefine my lips. She had forgotten hers and reached over to borrow mine. I love being a grown-up, and sharing lipstick with my mother.

31

Between
Stuff and Rescue

~

I watch TV. I know that isn't very scholarly or spiritual. TV is banal, and basically junk food for the soul. I even have a good friend who wrote a book on why it is bad to watch too much TV. But I watch TV.

I really like the Discovery Channel. I've actually learned a lot about the migration of polar bears and how much food the mother bear has to eat before she hibernates each year so she can keep warm and survive until the next spring. And I once watched a special comparing the life expectancy of a young crocodile, "Cleo," with that of a young alligator, "Ally." It's amazing how many of them don't live past a few months. And don't get me going on that guy who hangs out with reptiles. He goes up and stands right next to a crocodile and says something like, "Ooh, she's a beaut! But don't let her silence fool you, she's quite deadly this one, she is. Let's get a bit closer, all right?" I am sitting on the edge of my seat by that time.

Now don't cluck your tongue at me. Like you never watch TV?

When I paint I'll keep the television on either the House and Garden Network or The Learning Channel. It's the strangest thing, but I have to have something occupying the verbal side of my brain (not so much that I have to really pay attention—in fact, shows with a plot are definitely out), so that I can comfortably access the creative side of my brain. If I don't have something keeping that hemisphere of the brain busy, I find that I begin thinking about things and start to dissect and solve problems I'm dealing with. Suddenly, I find I am no longer painting a face, but a blob with unusually repetitive brush strokes. So I watch TV.

TV also helps me keep track of time. I know that if *Bob* "I can fix any house" *Villa* is over, I've spent an hour working on whatever I've been painting. And I also know that when all the "how-to" shows are over, and *Rescue 911* is on, it's time to stop and eat dinner.

So one day when I was painting, day turned to night and *Rescue 911*. I was painting, but watching. *Rescue 911* is really quite compelling. So many people on the edge of life and death, and so many heroes ready to risk their lives to save them. This is the stuff of which great drama is made. So I watch.

After saving a woman from her car, which had crashed into an embankment and was hanging precariously over the edge of an overpass, they headed to the Midwest with the cameras. You see, a storm had come up and the local river crested way, way over flood stage and went crashing through the small town. People were being rescued from the tops of houses and trees everywhere. The water was raging like a rapid rider's dream. In the crisis of the moment, a helicopter was lowering a "rescue technician" in a harness to try and save a young boy stuck in the top of a tree. Now what I can't figure out is this: how did this kid get up in the tree…with his bicycle. But it is television, so I assume a little suspension of disbelief is required. Well, anyway, the guy is lowered within rescue distance and extends his hands to the boy. The boy reaches out with one arm and tries to grab the man, but no can do. This rescue will demand both hands from the boy, requiring that he let go of the bicycle. By this time, I have stopped painting and have surrendered my full attention to the drama unfolding on my cable channel.

For the next tenuous minutes, the rescuer attempts to convince the boy that he must let go of the bicycle if he is to be rescued. Right. This kid has a death grip on his bike. It has become more important to him than rescue. Or maybe, I think, he doesn't realize that he is facing a life or death choice. Mortality is such an abstract thought in contrast to this bicycle which is something he can touch and hold. And so it gives him a false sense of security, and he holds onto it with all of his nine-year-old strength, rejecting the rescuer's hands.

Well, the child is panicked, and there is no talking him out of the bike. Deciding there is no more time and no other choice, the rescuer straps a harness around the boy, and then his bike, and gives the signal to the winch operator to reel them in. I don't know much about the engineering of helicopters and their rescue ropes, but it seemed risky to hook a bicycle onto the bottom of the load. And evidently, it was. Just a few feet up the dangling bicycle began to spin, twirling the two attached human beings like eggs in a blender. The rescuer somehow managed to cut the bike loose, and the crew above pulled both him and the boy into the helicopter. Watching the heroic actions of the rescuer, I actually got a *Touched by an Angel* tear in my eye.

Being the contemplative that I am, I really saw a whole lot in this TV show. While I recognize that *Rescue 911* is not typically billed as a show for contemplatives, it all seemed so up front and on the plate.

When I am in need of rescue, what am I holding onto so tightly that I can't reach out and grab the Rescuer's hand?

What stuff in my life gives me a false sense of security? Sometimes it is significance and self-esteem. Sometimes it is relationships. Sometimes it is money, or even wisdom and knowledge. Whatever it is, in the midst of a crisis, it will not save me. But when I am between my own abilities and the hand of the Savior, it is sometimes hard to let go of what I know and instead reach out, trusting what I cannot see. If I sit too long in my dilemma, I will drown. Because the hand of the Savior calls for a two-handed response, my stuff must be cut loose.

I wonder what Peter had to let go of to walk on water? When he saw Christ challenging the laws of physics and nature as He casually took a water walk, Peter headed for the edge of the boat. At the Master's invitation, he threw one foot over the side. I wonder if he considered grabbing a flotation device to take with him. Or maybe a video camera to record his historic moment? Or did he strap his own ego and confidence to his back before throwing the other foot over the side? Whatever it was he took with him, it weighed him down and caused him to start to sink shortly into his stroll. He must have had an instant underwater epiphany, because he let go of whatever it was and reached for the hand of Christ to save his life. Faithfully, the Rescuer had already reached for his.

It's not that bicycles are bad. Or any of the other stuff. They have their place and usefulness. But they can't walk on water. And when walking on water is required, I want to be holding onto the Water Walker with both hands.

And they say television is worthless...

32

Between Seasons

~

The garden has begun to take its bows. It has performed maturely. Not too showy, but consistent bundles of bushy brown-eyed Susans, floating white spots of tiny daisies, and polite purple lavender that accents without feeling the need to overwhelm. I have watered, cajoled, mulched, and fed, and now there is nothing to do but watch and wait. It is too early for pruning and cutting down, tying back and covering over. It is too late for fertilizing and propagating. But still my muddy black shoes, with the backs smashed down like an old man's slippers, sit at the ready beside gloves that are permanently shaped to my own hands. I sit and watch helplessly as the summer heat turns the leaves brown, knowing that as the stalks decapitate themselves, it is as it should be.

I have never exactly been a morning person, but I'm generally pleasant. Well, maybe pleasant is being too generous.

Let's just say I have made a deal with morning over the years that if she will announce herself gently, I will not skip her altogether. But lately, when the sun steals up the edges of my sleep-visor and rudely peels up my eyelids one eyelash at a time, I can't find the desire to begin the day. The intrusion of life, dragging her unfulfilled expectations before me, again drives me burrowing for another place in my sleep, one that is safer.

So I brace myself up with routines. Nine Frosted Mini-Wheats in a bowl with just enough skim milk to wet them all. Eat. Rinse dish, place it in the dishwasher. Visit the garden, pull any rampant weeds. Proceed to the bathroom for a preliminary session, the second to follow in approximately one hour. Good girl. You could stop now and have had a productive day. Except there are the other 15 hours and 45 minutes of waking to fill. And so the day begins. For some reason, it still seems that the morning freshness has become a bitter reminder that life is not as it should be. All my long-term plans for accomplishing great things and enjoying the view drip like maple syrup from my fingers, and I am torn between washing them clean and licking them dry. Things change. But so slowly that I sometimes feel as if years are passing between my breaths.

By evening, I have made peace with the day. So I reach for my sleep-visor, and burrow once again into my safe place.

When I was five, I was given a wagon-red bicycle with training wheels on it. My father was in Viet Nam, but three of my uncles were present. Christmas morning, I rode my vision of freedom down to my cousins' house where all of the uncles were waiting. With one uncle stationed at the rear, and one on each side, by the afternoon I had doggedly mastered forward motion on two tires and discarded the training wheels like a walking man's crutches. I was now an official mobile human being, the transformation taking only one warm Memphis Christmas Day.

Transformations take longer now. There is more waiting.

If someone hasn't said it to you or you haven't read it somewhere lately, *life passes like seasons*. There. I've stated the obvious. While the obvious is obvious, it isn't always an easy place to live. Like the heartfelt penned encouragements to "stay sweet and never change" from my 1976 senior yearbook, this observation doesn't tell me how to do it. How can we cope with a life that changes like seasons, and still stay sweet? Stating the obvious will at least give us a framework to start from.

I think that seasons are lovely, each with their own personalities. But sometimes waiting for the next one to come can seem interminable. Spring and fall seem to be the popularly longed-for changes. I have usually had enough of the extremes of mufflers, layers, and hot tea or picnics, spaghetti straps, and lemonade by the time the new temperatures finally come along. It is not the inevitability of change that I struggle with so much as it is the in-between. The passage. The getting there. And the thing is, I've been on this planet more than 40 years, and I ought to know and trust by now that spring will always come after winter. But existentially, it's harder to trust that rhythm.

There are so many in-betweens. Waiting for change to come sometimes leaves me feeling as though I am in suspended animation. Am I wasting away here God, waiting to discover the next phase of my life?

Those waiting to finally conceive a child cry out of the emptiness of their heart and womb, "When Lord, when?" Singles looking for their life-mate feel lost among the younger singles and lost among the marrieds. It's like adolescent purgatory, when we were neither child nor adult. The in-betweens of life commit to neither side of the page. Neither day or night, neither good or bad, neither waking nor sleeping, neither doubt or faith. Just in-between.

This is transition. Waiting. It is easy to allow the flesh-and-blood restrictions of time to defeat us or make us feel as though we are in an endless holding pattern. But waiting is not wasted time. It is a hiccup, or a parenthetical phrase. It is a pause, but it is not wasted. Waiting is becoming. And sometimes, it just takes time.

So I will occupy the moment. This season. I'll make it a season for rest, reflection, and reappropriating myself. I'll remember the blooms of summer while I enjoy the leaves of fall. And then the raw and exposed branches of winter. Then the explosion of spring. My shoes and gloves will sit at the ready for planting season next spring, but for now, the door will stay closed, for a season.

33

Between Months

~

There is a "K" on the calendar for this Wednesday. Every month of the year since I was seventeen has had a "K" on one day. That's because I am a woman. And my name is "Kim."

It's just another one of those clever codes we women have for notating "that time of the month." The Curse. Having a period. One's cycle. There are so many code names to describe this season of pain and distress women share each month. Some people think it is an easy excuse for women to eat chocolate and be cranky. Of course my response is, *since when do we need an excuse?* But aside from the culinary cravings and princess complex, there is a very real reality to our monthly struggle.

Pharmaceutical companies and therapists have capitalized on the woes of PMS and raging hormones. Comedians, advertisers, and self-help authors exploit the monthly plight, and early Jewish men would have preferred being a dog to being an "unclean" woman.

G. Campbell Morgan wrote that the sentence on the woman for her choice to sin in the Garden is that in the "distinctive exercise of her nature...she shall be wrapped in sorrow." I believe this includes the entire fertility package. From the first day a woman's body is able to produce a child, she begins to carry new sorrow. And whether she is longing for a child, happy to have a child, or just plain old menstruating, her body experiences sorrow on a monthly basis.

With the package comes our distinctly female emotions and sensitivities. I mean, my husband doesn't cry like I do when TV news programs show starving children. As much as he cares about them, he doesn't ache down deep for them the way I do. When my dear friend lost her mother, while Jim was very empathetic, he didn't cry with her at her loss. And I never find him curled in a ball sobbing about so many of our friends whose marriages are falling apart.

I'm not trying to glorify my extreme feelings or in some way portray women as martyrs. I'm just trying to illustrate Mr. Morgan's statement that we will be "wrapped in sorrow." It is part of the price a woman pays for the collateral of original sin.

Men have their own collateral from the fall in issues of significance and fear of failure, but they don't experience it monthly or mark it on the calendar with a "K" or something.

Our bodies, as women, retain not only water each month, but the sting of disobedience. The entire process of childbearing was originally never intended to be anything but joyous from conception to delivery.

I have had friends through the years who desperately wanted to have children. But with each passing month, the emptiness inside grew exponentially as home pregnancy test after home pregnancy test came back negative. And while they fought through their own pain to celebrate the birth of other couples' babies, they experienced longings that only Sarah could understand. Or perhaps Hannah, or Rebecca, or Elizabeth. Women who lamented to God their deepest longings to bear children.

I can't give a profound theological treatise on why women who long to have children don't conceive, but I have to believe from Scripture that it wasn't intended to be that way. To believe that God intended for every woman who longed to become a mother to bear children easily and painlessly is not a stretch for me. But to believe that as a result of original sin the course God first intended for us has been altered is also not a stretch for me.

It just leaves me silent when I sit with my yearning and disappointed friends each month.

The pharmaceutical companies cannot produce something to fix that. And in truth, bearing a child will not actually "fix" the deep wound. Just the same, I don't understand why some people seem to have children by barely even thinking about it, and some suffer anguish for empty months with empty wombs. Or why some people carry children only to lose them. Or why every month I fight the blues, crankiness, and general wretchedness. But as with all the results of sin, they must be carried and deposited at the feet of the wounded Savior, who chose to bleed for our redemption. And who promised not once, but every time we need it, to collect us up and hold us close.

I am reminded of the deep cost of sin at least every 30 days or so. A "K" on my calendar reminds me. And I am grateful for the forgiving Savior who never lets go of us, and who is the only one we can turn to to fill our longings and soothe our aches.

But for your own safety, you might want to steer clear of me for the next week or so. At least until the crankiness subsides.

34

Between Worlds

~

*I*t is not really the tears that exhaust me, but rather the hopeless feeling out of which they are born. If God really does collect our tears in a bottle, I hope He was able to locate an empty vat lying around heaven for mine.

I was making some calls the other day, and at one point the person on the other end picked up and said, "We're having a great day at the Christian Center, how about you?" Now, I'm a good girl, really. But the hairs on the back of my neck stood up so strong that they made me think bad-girl thoughts. The flippant joy being announced by the perky voice on the other end of the phone left an acrid odor in my flaring nostrils.

Joy does not come to me that way. It's not a mantra I repeat or a candy treat I can pop in my mouth. Joy lives next door to deep, dark, unspeakable emptiness. It is the flip side of despair and is sometimes delicate and fragile. Its seeming inaccessibility causes me to feel shame for not being able to tap into the joy of my salvation.

What more could I want? I have a magazine-picture life. A merciful Savior graced me with love and forgiveness, a deeply wise and lovingly faithful husband, a charming cottage home in a stimulating section of town, a career that allows me to express myself through the arts that I love so much, health for me and those I care about...so why am I not "having a great day at the Christian center"? And the even deeper question: Why does it irritate me that someone else is?

In his book, *The Call*, Os Guinness writes about the noonday demon of slothfulness, describing it not so much as laziness, but as a state of emptiness and desperation. He refers to Vaclav Havel's writing on "The temptation of Nothingness..." I fight this demon. The French term *ennui* describes it best for me, implying a boredom or lack of zest for life. A long yawn. And it feels like it is spiritual ennui that seizes up the engines of joy and motivation inside of me.

I look at the garden in my backyard that once provoked me to childlike enthusiasm. Now, I just think it's too hot to go outside and there are too many bugs to make it even worth getting all dirty. The drawings and canvases that wait in my studio used to hold my focus until I would suddenly look at the clock and discover that day had become night had become morning. Now I step by the doorway wanting to be seized by the muse, but pass by unmotivated, letting my work sit untouched. Friends call to invite me to lunch and a wander in one of our favorite antique stores, but I let my answering machine communicate that I'm unavailable. Oh, I'm unavailable all right. Unavailable to friends, myself, and it seems to any movement of the Spirit. I am a slug.

I find myself between youthful optimism that told me anything was possible if you just worked hard at it, and the wisdom of age that helps you see what is worth working for and what the true definitions of *reward* and *success* are. My ideals and unbordered dreams have faced the cold-shower reality of midlife, and so I wait for the grace and wisdom that come with time to restart the deeper engines of spiritual hunger in me.

It has reached epidemic proportions in my world. It seems as though everyone I know is in this lethargic state of unbeing. Another French term, *laissez-faire,* is so appropriate; "who could care?" What is a midlife crisis if not a recognition that all the things we thought would bring fulfillment don't? Most of my friends are in a desperate time of reevaluating. While it seems that women are more in tune with these waves of ennui, even a lot of the men I know are expressing the same feeling of "so what," and mourn in the emptiness that plagues their accomplishments. Too many of my married friends are bored with their marriages and are disposing of them. And what about the general malaise of the country at large? In a normal national presidential election, less than 50 percent of the eligible voting public usually vote to elect the most important and influential leader in the world. In spiritual circles, the popularity of production-heavy, entertainment-oriented churches that demand nothing more than Sunday spectatorship hints at a spiritual boredom too.

We are uninterested, unmotivated, and uninspired. And so we slink into the lethargy of futility. It slowly chokes the life out of us. In fact, I've been waiting to write this chapter for months. I kept thinking I would get to the other side in time to yell instructions back over my shoulder. But here I sit, still in the mud, gasping for air. Still a slug.

Qoheleth, "the Teacher" (probably King Solomon) is credited with writing the book of Ecclesiastes in the Old Testament. He was also a slug. Sometimes he had a few instructions to shout over his shoulder, but the fact that he was mostly slug comforts me. He laments the "vanity" of life more than 30 times in 12 concise chapters. I picture him walking around in his bathrobe, a two-day growth on his chin, and a half-eaten pint of ice cream on his bedside table. His book is, almost to the page, exactly halfway between Genesis and Revelation. Midway between creation and the culmination of history. A biblical midlife crisis. I know, I am hearing true Bible scholars remind me that the Bible is not necessarily in chronological order. But I dare you to take away the significance of the fact that this midlife crisis of Qoheleth's is divinely set midway between the historic recording of our birth and homecoming. You can't. Because God is very clever that way, and He knew that people like me who look for things like that would be incredibly comforted by discovering it.

Qoheleth declares that everything in life is vanity. In the Hebrew this word means a mere breath, a vapor. Transience. Emptiness. Futility. It seems that Qoheleth spoke the deepest thoughts of my soul. Derek Kidner (*The Wisdom of Proverbs, Job & Ecclesiastes*) suggests that the Teacher was speaking of the missing element of "forever" that God made man conscious of. It is this missing element, this ungraspable sense of eternity, that we long for and that causes us to feel the vanity of the brief satisfactions of this world.

I don't know that it was ever intended to be this way. This may be my own little theological/poetical/hormonal assumption, but I wonder if when we ate from the forbidden tree of knowledge, we exposed ourselves to this life-stealing cancer. It seems true that the more we understand, the more pain and difficulty we experience.

When he has not given in to the fleeting satisfaction of hedonism as the only joy on earth, in his moments of understanding Qoheleth shouts back some instructions for those of us coming after him. He simply states what Augustine later borrowed from him, that we are going to be restless until we find our rest in God alone. The fear of God; for *this* is every man made. This is the closest we can come to *olam*, the antithesis of vanity. Our search must not be for meaning, but for the God who gives meaning. Happiness can't be achieved, it must be received. The God who planted eternity in our hearts is the only one who can satisfy our deepest longings. C. S. Lewis has said that if nothing in this world satisfies us, we must conclude we were made for another world. And "in order to be prepared to hope in what does not deceive, we must," as Georges Bermanos has said, "first lose hope in everything that deceives."

I don't know exactly what this all looks like when lived out in our skin. But I'm trying. Further on in the New Testament I find the distinct statement of hope that creation, which has been subjected to futility, will be set free from the slavery of this hollow pursuit (see Romans 8). But it is a hope unseen that we must trust in.

All is from God, and in God. Joy and fulfillment are not something I can conjure up, or work up, or do. They are only in the hands of the One whose grasp is eternal.

When a mirror is held up to our life and pursuits, the only thing it will show us is our breath, and even that too is borrowed from Him who made us. Between worlds, we must rely on temporary breaths of heaven to sustain us, and long for the eternal breath of God that we will one day share in His presence.

A slug is a sort of cousin to a caterpillar (in a poetical/hormonal sense). And we all know what happens to the caterpillar in transition.

For now, we sit and wait in our slug-ness, anticipating our transformation. Between this world and the one we were made for.

35

Between Breaths

~

I have walked for 40 minutes every morning for three or four years now. Not "every" every morning, but most mornings. Sometimes not on Sundays. Or days when I was too busy. Or when it rained. But enough mornings that I feel confident in loosely using the term "every."

Enough mornings that I am deeply resenting the fact that after climbing the stairs in the Royal Albert Hall at a pretty quick pace, by the time I got to my seat in the "outer-atmosphere row," I couldn't get my breath. My mother, who doesn't walk every morning, was sitting beside me, and I couldn't decide whether she or I would need defibrilating first. Isn't this why I walk every morning? So that when I am exerting myself in public places I will not appear to also be dying?

The deal is that when I finally catch my breath, it's gone and I'm in pursuit of another. Is this some dog-chasing-tail joke perpetuated on my respiratory system? Is there actually a way to catch my breath, or is it like trying to hold "now" from becoming "then"? I mean, by the time I say "now" it is "was."

In some form, the rhythm of my breathing and the pursuit of another breath is a time-marker. As each breath is anticipated in the future, found in the now, and finished in the past, a chronological event of respiratory function is measured. I am told that these sort of internal clocks regulate our behavior.

Animals and plants are also governed by internal clocks. Leaves of leguminous plants lie in one position during the day and another at night. Sea anemones expand and contract to the rhythm of the tides, bees come for food at fixed periods of time, and humans can estimate time without the help of clocks or sensory clues. Norbert Wiener, a U.S. mathematician, speculates that our sense of time might depend on the rhythm of certain electrical oscillations in the brain.

And, I add, maybe by the measuring of our breaths.

For convenience, the world has adopted a universal form of time measurement. Since A.D. 1600, the 24-hour day, 60-minute hour, and 60-second minute has been in general use. Even more particular, the adoption of the mean solar day, which is comprised of 86,400 seconds, has defined time. Thinking about this gives me a new appreciation for, or obsession with, how I use my time.

These specific measurements give us the basis for the development of the calendar. And the calendar gives us a means of reckoning time in divisions and periods. These are necessary for the recording of history. This is *chronos*, a linear definition of time.

This definition has created an entire industry of calendars, Day Timers, Palm Pilots, Post-its, watches, clocks, and other time-capturing devices. And an entire culture of overworked, overstressed, overcommitted husks of people.

In this linear definition of time I am trying to understand and make sense of the Alpha and Omega, the Beginning and the End. The Eternal Now, who was and is and is to come.

I'm trying to break time down into smaller pieces. Right now, I want to just live in the moment with the God who is also known as "I Am."

Interestingly enough, knowing I Am even in the moment is still frustrating. Much like trying to catch one's breath, or tail. Just when I capture a little of it, it has passed, and I am off in pursuit again. It's like looking at the North Star, or Venus, or Mars. Just when I think I see them, they blend into the dusk that straddles night. And in the times that I get a glimpse of I Am, when I begin to feel the heat from the flames of the Glory of God that lick at the altar of my water-doused heart, my wandering eye extinguishes them before I am consumed.

And I am in pursuit again. Frustrated by *chronos*. Between breaths still.

Even though I don't have a watch, or calendar, or clock that can measure it, I am more than positive that God's time is not like ours. How can He be Was, Is, and Is to Come all at once in a *chronos* sequential measuring of time? Is it not because He is beyond our four space-time dimensions? The Eternal Now measures time in *kairos*. This Greek word

174 ～ Living in the Sacred Now

implies the exact time appointed to something. In *kairos* it is as if time is completely unbounded, yet also stopped. Only in *kairos* can He be one, yet three. Only in His time can free will and predestination exist simultaneously. Only in His time can He know me before I am.

The distinction between *chronos* and *kairos* is easier for me to see drawn on paper. *Chronos* would be illustrated by one straight line going forward, its end known only in God's mind. On it, you can see past events, present events, and anticipated future events. It is linear. However, *kairos* is the abstract artist's dream. Lines, circles, arcs going in all directions. Both now *and* then. Both here *and* there. It's sort of like the way a child colors before they become self-conscious and careful about staying inside the lines. In this wonderful jumble of marks that pays no heed to dimensions, God is both near and yet far. And when I forget to pray today about something and instead pray about it tomorrow, it is within God's time to have heard my prayer tomorrow as today. Madeleine L'Engle suggested that in God's time, freed of the normal restrictions of our linear time, we can even "experience in a few chronological seconds years of transfigured love." I am becoming in *chronos*, I am complete in *kairos*.

There is an entire world of science and philosophy that studies issues of particle physics, quantum physics, time-space relativities, and dimensional conundrums. In this world of multisyllable concepts, scientists have come to the conclusion that the mass density of the universe is *exactly* what it needs to be to sustain human life. If the mass density were too great, too much deutrium would be produced and the stars would burn out too quickly. If the mass density were too little, there would be too little deutrium and helium to sustain the heavier elements necessary for life.

I am not wired for that kind of thinking. The scientist's eye sees minutiae that I can barely even imagine. What I can understand is that when God said, "Let there be light," the sky was filled with the approximately hundred million trillion stars necessary to sustain life in our universe. He said, "Let there be light" on the first day of history, but in *kairos*, He has said it today as well.

In *kairos*, today, He says "let us make Kim in our image," and "come unto Me," and "don't be anxious."

And while I am between breaths in *chronos*, in *kairos* He has just breathed the first and everlasting breath into my being on the first day of the beginning.

36

Between
Starting and Finishing

~

*T*he romance of absolutely anything will fade. If you don't believe me, then you are probably in denial or you haven't lived long enough. The romance of the first day of school is only matched by the last day. The first snow is intoxicating, the last is victory. But all the days of school and all the snows between the first and the last eventually become a matter of routine and discipline to get through.

Running in a marathon starts with excitement and ends with adrenalin. Between starting and finishing, I'm told that the fifteenth to eighteenth miles of a 25-mile marathon are the hardest. You have no starting line or finishing line in sight and progress seems unmeasurable. But the race is won or lost in those miles.

The excitement of a new marriage and the adventure of two lives blending together has a great start. Toothpaste battles, toilet seat ups and downs, sharing a sink, and financial disagreements don't dampen the fire of passion in the first few years. At the other end, couples who have been married for decades have worked through the middle years and now enjoy the security and comfortableness of well-worn companionship. But in between, the songs of duet living are not always harmonious. The progress towards oneness seems negligible.

The birth of a baby is met with excitement. At first, the mesmerizing little life captures every waking moment of the parents' most willing and complete attention. But somewhere between diapers and college, the zeal fades and the task becomes draining. Days turn into weeks, weeks turn into months, with no measurable signs of progress other than outgrown shoes and clothes.

Starting a new job is usually filled with possibility and second chances. But before the fulfillment of retirement, it becomes bland and uninspiring. Sustaining the sense of progress and forward movement gets bogged down in middle management purgatory.

Starting and finishing something seems to be where the satisfaction is. Grand openings and going-out-of-business sales. Bon voyages and welcome homes. Weddings and fiftieth anniversary parties. But what about all the time between starting and finishing?

I know this experience best in my art studio. When I start a painting, the blank canvas incites me to work. The expectation of creation drives my hand. I'll skip meals and bathroom breaks, consumed by the joy of my craft. Sleep becomes a nonessential, and I am myopic in my focus. But midway through, between the joys of starting and finishing the painting, an attack of lethargy usually threatens my progress. Decisions on color, shape, and placement become daunting, and inspiration is muffled. Naps become more frequent and interruptions more welcome.

It is in those times that I have to trust the process to produce progress. Even when it seems as though I'm making no progress, I have to faithfully stand in front of the canvas and apply paint, trusting that with each diligent stroke, I am one stroke closer to completion. Sometimes I just have to do the things I know in my head instead of waiting for the jolts of inspiration, because it is by the faithful application of each layer of paint that the painting makes its way to the edges of the canvas. And to its completion.

There is a scientific term referred to as JND, meaning "Just Noticeable Difference." It is the minimum detectable difference brought about by a minimum amount of stimulus. Big changes are easy to note, but researchers needed a way to note the smallest ones. This necessity prompted a group of German scientists to come up with the "Natural Law of Just Noticeable Difference." In the end, a collection of JNDs are equally as important to the overall result as are large and distinct differences. In our lives, it is persistence in the barely discernible steps of progress that takes us from start to finish. While we want to see the same sort of excitement and satisfaction found in starting, it is the JNDs that will get us to finishing.

So it is in my faith life. Coming to know Christ brings with it all the zeal of young faith. My devotion to Christ and my surrender to His direction is unquestioning. This is the "He walks with me, and He talks with me" honeymoon of faith. Upon finishing, my arrival in heaven will bring with it a completeness unknowable before then. The joy will be unending, beyond my own imagining, and there will be no sorrow or disappointment. But between starting and finishing the life of faith, what sustains the joy of my salvation? How will I continue to move toward Him? After the initial stirring, what will urge me forward? In the words of A. W. Tozer, "To have found God and still to pursue Him is the soul's paradox of love..."

The barely discernible efforts that produce barely discernible progress are what I am called to. The accumulation of these will urge me forward. It is great when—and if—days come that are filled with wide-eyed revelation. But there will be more days of barely discernible progress than those of epiphanic proportions. Our culture would have us believe that isn't enough. And so would many well-meaning people of faith. I'm not saying that we should just sit back and surrender to lethargy or uninspired faith. But the measure of our faith is not found in grandiose happenings. Peter walked on the water, but only once. The rest of his life he was faithful to simple land walking.

Land walking is made up of hundreds of JNDs, one step after the other. Sometimes through mud, sometimes through dry-bones dust. Although it may seem sometimes as if the horizon is moving away from us, when we look over our shoulder at the end of the day, we'll see that we aren't where we used to be.

Between starting and finishing, that is what will sustain us.

37

Between
Malachi and Matthew

~

God, sometimes I just want to hear Your voice. I want to know that You hear mine. And even though faith is believing without actually hearing, seeing, smelling, tasting, or touching, I still want to.

Once in a while, when I have been emptying my heart in Your presence, I feel foolish. Because You never actually say anything. And here I am, rambling on and on about the captions and headlines of my day, lost in a shameless self-absorbed rant. In fact, as I download my wants, I can easily be deluded into thinking that Your greatest desire is for my happiness. That distortion must sound like shrieking in Your ear. But still You are silent. I would love to elicit even a slight "Hmmm."

My own silent experience is not unique. Between the writing of Malachi and Matthew, heaven was silent for 400 years. The pillar of cloud had dispersed and the pillar of fire had burned out. There were no voices or tablets from the mountaintops, no prophets commanding fire down to lick up a saturated altar, and no depressive lamentations of storm and stress like those of Jeremiah. And no still, small voice.

There was not even a slight "Hmmm."

It seems there are many occasions for silence. Especially before something significant happens. And after those 400 years of silence, heaven and earth suddenly rang with "Gloria in excelsis Deo" and the Son of God was announced, the coming Emmanuel. But when the echo died down, there began 30 more years of silence.

Other than a report of a brief childhood encounter at the temple, we hear nothing of Jesus until a voice arose from the silence in the wilderness. The servant John shouted, preparing the way for the Savior Son. And then, at the Baptism of Jesus, heaven broke the silence again.

Even with the Savior's arrival though, it wasn't the last time for silence. After three intense years of teaching, healing, and calling, Jesus told His disciples of His impending death. The declaration of His appointment with the cross crushed the disciples. "Gloria in excelsis" a fading refrain, six days of silence ensued.

In anticipation of the crucifixion, Jesus took time in Gethsemane to beseech heaven. He laid His soul bare, and cried, and agonized to His Father. We're told that He even sweat beads of blood. This rare but documented medical condition is called *hemohydrosis*. It occurs in cases of extreme stress or shock, when a person's capillaries become weakened and bleed into the sweat pores. Blood and water mingle on the surface of the skin. When this happened to Jesus, it was not during a passing prayer for traveling mercy, but in the midst of an agonizing storming of heaven.

Even for Jesus, heaven remained silent.

Likewise, the psalmist begged God to wake up. To not be silent. To come to his defense and contend for him (Psalm 35). Don't be silent and still (Psalm 83). But when God interrupts the silence, it is at His will. He will not be tamed or invoked like a magic genie.

I think I have usually equated "silence" with "abandonment." The moments that echo with nothing seem so lonely. My monologues feel unheard, and my letters of supplication seem to collect, unopened. In my most desperate times, I wonder if I cry alone.

But I know that when Jesus prayed in the garden, the silence from heaven did not indicate disregard or desertion on God's part. Nor did God relinquish the desire for His people for 400 years in the silence between Malachi and Matthew. And when the psalmist or I beg for Him to speak, He does not simply turn His back in indifference.

A taciturn heaven can be pregnant with Presence. And perhaps the silence is like that in Revelation after the seventh seal was broken, a certain hush before the trumpets.

God, in the nearly final words of Malachi, before the 400 years of silence, it says You heard, and that those who thought on Your name were written in Your book of remembrance. No, silence does not mean abandonment. You have collected my heart and words in golden bowls and they sit ever in Your presence.

I am listening. My ear is pressed to the door, and I'm listening. I'm anticipating the trumpets after the silence. Ready for You to speak in soul-stirring interruptions. Or even slight "Hmmms." And call me to life, faith, belonging.

38

Between the
Tomb and the Womb

~

I have felt a pause in my life. The forward movement has slowed to an unsettling dirge, with
strong indications of a complete ceasing of movement pending.

I'm flying home tonight, and as I look out the small airplane window beside me I see an endless darkness. There is
a little bit of light from some scattered stars, but they are far
enough away as to be negligible in effect. When I look hard
into this night sky, the darkness resonates, and it startles me
to realize that I am more at home in the dark than in the
brightness of day.

The dark passage of transition is inevitable in life. There
will be many such passages. But it would seem to me that a
mature recognition of their inevitability should entitle one to

185

a speedy resolution. Instead, I feel a slow and systematic shutting down of myself. And there is too much smell of death.

The death of friends' marriages. Too many of them. I was counting on their covenants of forever.

The death of youth. I don't like discovering a new ache or a less than fully functional bodily system every couple of days. I took it for granted all these years that I could turn a cartwheel on demand. But my cartwheel abilities are dead now. And so is some of the self-confidence and self-awareness that were givens in my youth.

The death of innocence. I don't mean this melodramatically. I just mean that I used to think that ultimately, when pushed, people would eventually choose to do what is right. That love and kindness could be appealed to so that people would do right and things would go well. This naive perspective has also died. People, including myself, are sinners in need of a Savior, and we do ugly things.

Death of dreams, death of the Disney paradigm, death of friendships, death of opportunities and the death of "change the world" energy.

There is a loneliness in this small and dark place. There is a feeling of waiting, waiting for the next season. And the waiting room looks suspiciously like a tomb.

I wonder if the chubby lime green caterpillar thinks of her chrysalis as a tomb. Does she know that she must, in essence, die before the luna moth can emerge? The dark closed-in space of the pupa could seem very tomb-like, if it weren't even more womb-like.

In the close safety of the cocoon, the pupa slowly surrenders and the plump earthbound caterpillar gives way to the lovely airborne luna moth. Nocturnal and fluorescent green, her four-inch wingspan lifts her to sights she would never have seen in her former self.

I was forwarded an email story of a man who came upon a chrysalis on his morning walk. He picked it up and set it in his office on his desk. He watched for any signs of emergence and saw nothing for days. The little package had more signs of death than life.

Finally it began to rock and stir. Inside, the butterfly was throwing herself against the wall of her cocoon in an attempt at rebirth. Finally the man couldn't stand it any longer and was compelled to help her. He got out some scissors and carefully clipped open the cocoon. Out tumbled a beautiful butterfly with two lovely wings, wings she had patiently grown in the darkness of her silent passage. But they were wings that would never carry her skyward, because part of the development of wings is in the struggle to exit the cocoon.

Possibly, I am, in my dark passage, growing wings for the next phase of my journey. Death is a part of transition, but it is a death unto life.

Sue Monk Kidd says the key to our times of transition is in letting our tombs be transformed into wombs. Places of becoming. Places of change and metamorphosis.

Christ has said that if we are to find our life, we must lose it (Matthew 16:25). And that if we are in Christ, we become new creatures (2 Corinthians 5:17). The caterpillar dies to become the butterfly. The seed dies to become the sapling. And while I am feeling stripped bare, exposed and raw in the silence of my dark passage, I will also become. God will take my shut-down soul and transform it.

I must sit still in the process and see this time of in-between as sacred, not wasted. It is the tomb become the womb. It is divinely ordered and directed. It is time that is preordained and directed by a God who wants to see me grow. And I must not rush it. Because in rushing the process, I might miss out on the necessary struggle, costing me the benefits of my fully grown new wings.

The Sweet
Now and Now

~

A this point, I suppose it's clear that it is between here and there that real life is lived. By the time we get "there," it becomes the new "here" and there is a new "there." In other words, rarely are we anywhere but in-between. Always in process, always in flux. Change is inevitable.

Before she died, my mother's mother, Nanny, made several quilts. I was given the last one. She couldn't bear to let all the scraps of fabric she had go to waste. So there, in the crudely sewn blanket, is a collection of my history. Patches from Barbie clothes she had made for me. Patches from dresses and skirts. Leftovers from clothes she had made for my cousin and for herself. Patches that symbolized various times in my life. The memories and the colors are equally stained into the cloth. And her tiny hand stitches are the connective tissue that hold it all together.

God saves our "nows" to create the picture of our life. Quilts that tell stories of our progress. His Holy Spirit weaves our experiences together as the connective tissue of our becoming. When we step back to look, if we see through the eyes of faith, sometimes it begins to make sense. Each small patch connects to the next until, at the end of our journey, there is a large multicolored blanket. Each of our "nows" is made more powerful by its connection to another. And on our homecoming, God wraps us in the completed quilt and welcomes us.

A friend called from the beach where he was on retreat this week to tell my husband and me about his Sunday church experience. He had decided to visit a local gathering of believers and sat inconspicuously in a pew, quietly expectant. Testimony time came, and a slender black woman stood up to speak. Slightly stooped by years, her voice was clear and audible. She testified:

> We must live in the sweet now and now, brothers and sisters, not just wait our lives away for the sweet by and by. We must live in the sweet now and now.

I think I got a witness. Amen.